鶴のおりがみBOOK
Crane Origami Handbook

| 英語 | 仏語 | 中国語 (繁体字) |
| English | Français | 中文（繁體） |

小林 一夫
Kazuo Kobayashi

二見書房

variety

連鶴と鶴のバリエーション
Renzuru and other variations

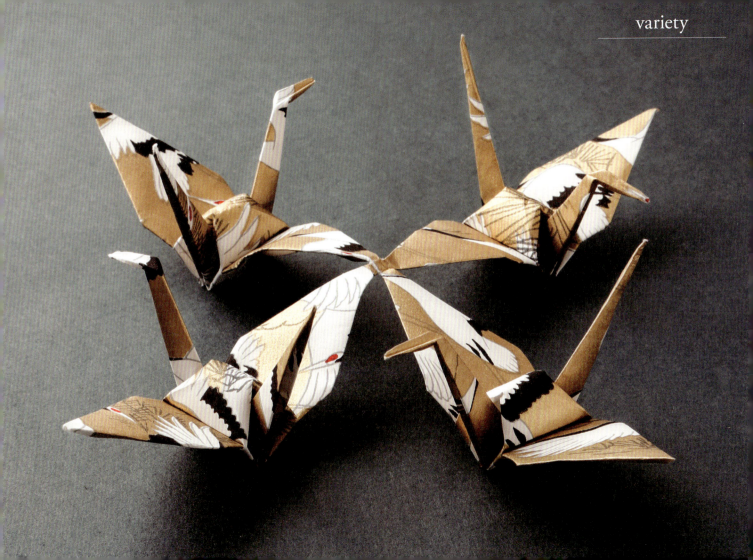

variety

variety

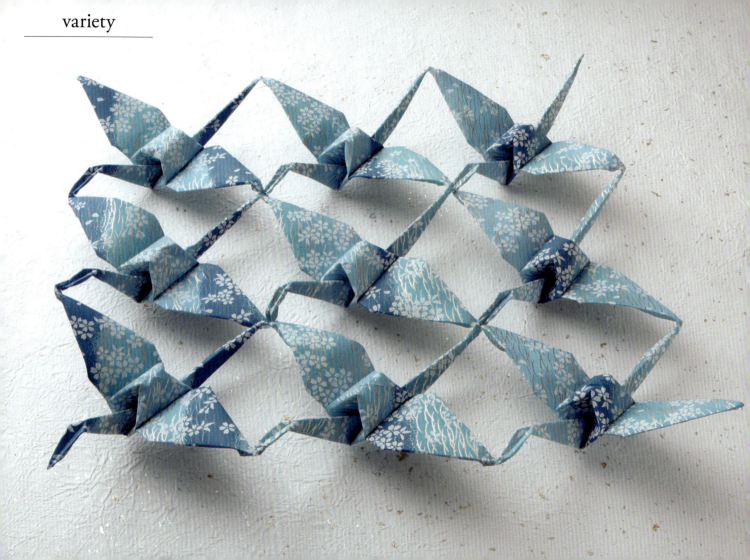

variety

event

お正月や節句を日本らしい折り鶴で
Celebrate the New Year and seasonal festivals with very Japanese paper cranes

event

tableware

美しい千代紙で食卓を彩って
Adorn your dining table with beautiful chiyogami paper

tableware

envelope

ぽち袋や祝儀袋を鶴の飾りで華やかに
Make gift envelopes stunning with decorative cranes

book&interior

読書タイムとインテリアを演出
Bring cranes onstage during reading time, or as a part of your interior design

CONTENTS

variety

恋鶴 Love Cranes	四連鶴 Quadruplet Cranes	青海波 Wave Pattern Cranes	基本の鶴 Basic Crane	はばたく鶴 Flapping Crane	二重の鶴 Double-Layered Crane	巣ごもり鶴 Nesting Crane
20	20	20	21	23	25	27

event

鶴の門松 Crane *Kadomatsu*	寿鶴A Congratulatory Crane A	寿鶴B Congratulatory Crane B	鶴のめびな Crane Empress Doll	鶴のおびな Crane Emperor Doll	端午の節句の鶴 Boys' Day Crane
29	31	33	35	37	39

はじめに Preface —— 14
折り鶴の話 The Story of the Paper Crane —— 15
基本の折り方 Basic Folds —— 18
きれいに折るコツ The Secret of Crisp Folds —— 19
折り方の記号 Folding Symbols —— 16
この本の使い方 Using this book —— 19
本書の作品の折り方 How to Fold Designs in This Book —— 65

tableware

鶴の器
Crane Bowl
41

小箱鶴
Small Box Crane
43

鶴の箸置き
Crane Chopstick Rest
45

鶴の懐紙
Crane *Kaishi*
47

envelope

鶴のたとう
Crane *Tatō*
49

鶴のぽち袋A
Crane *Pochi-bukuro* A
51

envelope

鶴のぽち袋B
Crane *Pochi-bukuro* B
53

お祝い鶴
Celebratory Crane
55

book & interior

鶴のブックマーカー
Crane Corner Bookmarks
57

鶴のしおり
Crane Bookmark
59

鶴のメモスタンド
Crane Note Stand
61

鶴の花入れ
Crane Vase
63

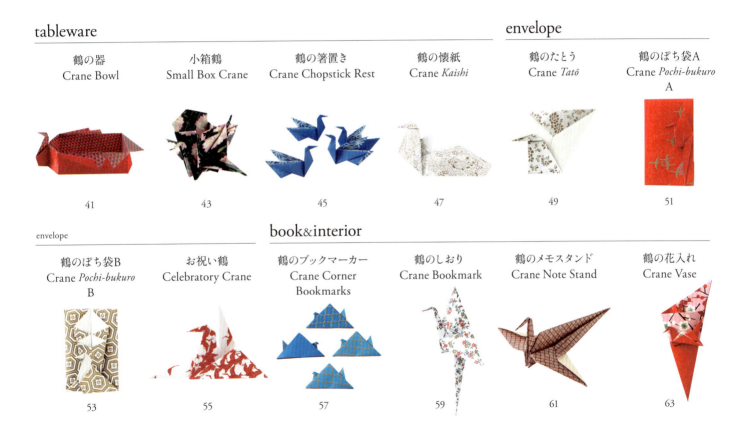

はじめに
Preface

　昔から千代紙には、動植物や風景、水や波、雲など、身近なモチーフが使われてきました。いろいろな由来から縁起がよいとされる吉祥紋もあり、図案化され組み合わされることで、美しい紋様として現代に伝わっています。「鶴は千年、亀は万年」といわれ、長寿の象徴でもある鶴も吉祥紋のひとつです。
　もともと鶴のモチーフは、中国でも長寿や戦勝の印として紋様となっており、そのうちの何種類かが日本に伝わっています。なかでも頭頂部が赤い丹頂鶴は、その姿や飛ぶさまが美しく、神の使いとして信仰の対象になっていました。現在も花嫁衣裳の打掛に描かれるなど、おめでたい行事に使われ、親しまれています。
　本書では、いろいろなタイプの折り鶴を紹介しています。千代紙もそれに合わせて、鶴をはじめとした吉祥紋や美しい図柄を載せていますので、千代紙ならではのデザインを楽しみながら折ってみてください。

小 林 一 夫

Since long ago, familiar motifs such as animals, plants, landscapes, water, waves, and clouds have been used for chiyogami paper. There are also symbols of various origins, said to be omens of good luck, and these have been designed and arranged into the beautiful patterns that we see today. It is said that "a crane lives a thousand years, a turtle, ten thousand years" – the crane, a symbol of longevity, is also one of these good omens.

Originally, the crane motif also symbolized longevity and victory in China, and some of the resulting patterns made their way to Japan. Particularly, the beauty of the red-crowned crane's shape and flight made it an object of faith as a godly messenger. Today as well, it is familiar to many, used in a number of special events – adorning the bridal robes worn over wedding kimono, for example.

In this book, we will introduce you to various types of folded paper cranes. We've also included chiyogami with auspicious motifs, including cranes, and other beautiful patterns as well, so please enjoy these distinctive designs with every fold.

Kazuo Kobayashi

折り鶴の話
The Story of the Paper Crane

　折り鶴は伊勢神宮の神事、儀礼から始まったといわれ、江戸時代には文化として広まりました。
　折り鶴の歴史でもっとも重要なものは、1797年に京都の吉野家為八によって発行された『秘傳千羽鶴折形』でしょう。木版一色刷りで49種の連鶴の紙の切り方に狂歌が添えられており、世界でもっとも古い折り紙本と考えられています。義道一円（魯縞庵）という桑名（三重県）のお坊さんが、集めた伝承の連鶴に自分の作品を付け加え、これを『東海道名所図会』などで知られる秋里籬島がまとめたとされています。本書に掲載している「青海波」も、この本に記されている連鶴のひとつです。
　折り鶴は子どもの遊びとして、また平和や幸福のシンボルとして、時代が変わっても形を変えることなく受け継がれてきています。

Paper cranes are said to have originated from the Shinto rituals and observances at Ise Grand Shrine, and spread as a part of Japanese culture in the Edo period.
The most important piece of the paper crane's history may be the book, Hiden Senbazuru Orikata ("Secret to Folding One Thousand Cranes"), published in 1797 by Yoshinoya Tamehachi in Kyoto. It is considered to be the oldest origami book in the world, containing single-color woodblock prints of instructions for how to cut 49 kinds of renzuru (connected cranes), accompanied by satirical poetry. It is said that a monk named Gidō Ichien (pen-name: Rokōan), from Kuwana (now Mie Prefecture) added his own work to a collection of traditional cranes, and this was compiled by Akisato Ritō, known for such works as Tōkaidō Meisho Zue ("Famous Places on the Tokaido Road"). The Wave Pattern renzuru design found in the collection is one we've chosen to include in this book.
The paper crane continues to be passed down – as a plaything for children, and as a symbol of peace and happiness – never changing its shape, even as the times change around it.

『秘傳千羽鶴折形』の複製
Reproduction of Hiden Senbazuru Orikata, one of the oldest known origami books

折り方の記号 Folding Symbols

線の種類や矢印など、この本で使う記号の説明をします。
記号は、折り図を見るときに必要になります。

This section describes types of lines, arrows and other symbols used in this book. You will need to understand these symbols when you view the Folding Diagrams.

紙の表と裏 Front and back of chiyogami paper

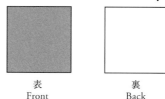

表
Front

裏
Back

谷折り Valley fold

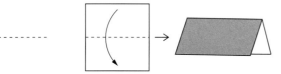

手前に折る
Fold towards yourself.

点線が内側になるように折る
Fold so that the dotted line is on the inside.

折り筋をつける Make a crease

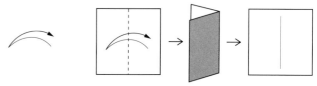

一度折って線をつけたあと、開いて元に戻す
Fold once to create a line in the paper and then unfold.

山折り Mountain fold

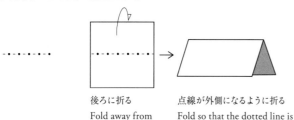

後ろに折る
Fold away from yourself.

点線が外側になるように折る
Fold so that the dotted line is on the outside.

矢印の方向に折る Fold in the direction of the arrow

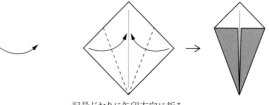

記号どおりに矢印方向に折る
Fold in the direction of the arrow as indicated by the symbol.

紙の向きを変える　Change the position of the paper

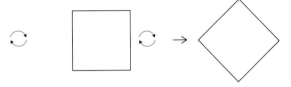

向きを変えたところ
New paper position.

紙の間を開く　Open up the space created by a fold

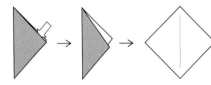

折った紙の間を開く
Open up the space between two or more layers of folded paper.

間を開いたところ
View of the space exposed by opening.

紙を裏返す　Turn the paper over

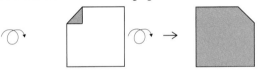

裏返したところ
View of the project after it is turned over.

ハサミで切る　Cut with scissors

 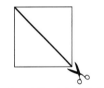

ハサミで切りこみを入れたり、切り落としたりする
Use scissors to make cuts and/or remove pieces of paper.

切ったところ
View after cutting.

図を拡大して示す　Enlarge the diagram

拡大したところ
Enlarged view.

同じ幅　Same width

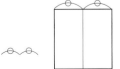

同じ角度　Same angle

基本の折り方 Basic Folds

複数の折り方に共通する、よく使う折り方の説明をします。
Let's learn several common folding techniques often used in origami.

段折り　Pleat Fold

1

山折りと谷折りをする
Make a mountain fold and valley fold.

2

できあがり
Finished!

巻き折り　Roll Fold

1

谷折りをくり返して、紙を巻くように折る
Repeat valley folds, and fold as if rolling up the paper.

2

できあがり
Finished!

中割り折り　Inside Reverse Fold

1

まとめて折り筋をつけてから、谷折りは山折りに変える
First make all creases, and then change the valley folds to mountain folds.

2

先端を内側に入れるように折る
Fold so that the tip is tucked inside the paper.

3

できあがり
Finished!

かぶせ折り　Outside Reverse Fold

1

折り筋をつける
Make a crease.

2

開いてかぶせるように折る
Open, and fold down to cover the paper.

3

できあがり
Finished!

この本の使い方
Using this book

- この本では、美しい千代紙を使って、25種類の「さまざまな鶴」や「鶴の小物」を折ることができます。
  With this book, you can fold 25 kinds of cranes and crane-inspired accessories, using beautiful chiyogami paper.

- キリトリ線で千代紙をカットして使います。なお、「恋鶴」「四連鶴」「青海波」用の千代紙はついていません。指定の大きさの紙を用意して折ってください。
  Please cut out the chiyogami along the dotted lines to use it. Chiyogami for the Love Cranes, Quadruplet Cranes and Wave Pattern Cranes is not included. Please prepare your own paper of the specified size to fold these designs.

- 折りたい作品を決め、p.66からの折り方を見ながら折ります。難易度を★の数で表わしているので、参考にしてください。
  Decide which design you'd like to make, and fold it according to the instructions starting on page 66. The number of stars (★) expresses the origami project's level of difficulty.

  ★☆☆ とても簡単 Simple
  ★★☆ ふつう Intermediate
  ★★★ 少し難しい Challenging

- 折り方のページには、英語のほかにフランス語、中国語（繁体字）も掲載しています。
  In the folding instructions, French and Chinese (traditional) are also provided in addition to English.

キリトリ線 — Cut Line
作品名 — Project
作品の解説 — Description
折り方のページ — Folding Instructions Page

紋様の名前 — Pattern
紋様の解説 — Pattern Description
キリトリ線（切ってから折る場合）— Cut Line (for *chiyogami* that is cut prior to folding)

きれいに折るコツ　The Secret of Crisp Folds

・角と角をきちんと合わせて折りましょう。Align corners precisely before you fold.
・折り筋はしっかりとつけましょう。Flatten fold edges until sharp and crisp.

20

こいづる
恋鶴
Love Cranes

1枚の紙から複数の鶴を折る連鶴には、さまざまな形があります。仲睦まじくクチバシでつながった2羽の鶴は、親子を表わした伝承の折形「拾餌(えひろい)」と同じつくりです。

There are various kinds of *renzuru*, connected cranes that can be made with one sheet of paper. These two affectionate cranes, connected by the beak, are made in the same way as the traditional parent-and-child design.

☞ p.68

よんれんづる
四連鶴
Quadruplet Cranes

連鶴ははじめに折り筋をつけ、切りこみを入れて折ります。紙を切り離さずに折るのが特徴。折り紙よりも切れにくい和紙で折るのがおすすめです。

Renzuru are made by first making creases, cutting and then folding. Cutting the paper without separating it completely is an important distinction. We recommend using washi, which is more difficult to cut than regular origami paper.

☞ p.70

せいがい は
青海波
Wave Pattern Cranes

鶴が連なって西方に飛ぶさまを表わした『秘傳千羽鶴折形(ひでんせんばづるおりかた)』にもある伝承の連鶴です。着物などにも見られる、古典紋様の青海波をイメージしています。

This traditional *renzuru* design depicts cranes flying in rows westward, and can also be found in *Hiden Senbazuru Orikata*. It calls to mind the classic wave pattern that can be seen decorating kimono and other objects.

☞ p.72

※「恋鶴」「四連鶴」「青海波」用の千代紙はついていません。指定の大きさの紙を用意して折ってください。
Chiyogami for the Love Cranes, Quadruplet Cranes and Wave Pattern Cranes is not included. Please prepare your own paper of the specified size to fold these designs.

基本の鶴
Basic Crane

折り紙の基本形として親しまれ、世界中に知られています。折り鶴は長寿や幸福、平和の象徴となる縁起物で、願いをこめて折ることもあります。

The basic paper crane design is familiar and well-known around the world. Paper cranes are lucky charms, symbolizing longevity, happiness, and peace, and are often folded while making a wish.

p.66

青海波
せいがいは
Wave Pattern

半円を幾重にも規則的に並べて、連なる波を表現した吉祥柄です。古代からある紋様ですが、源氏物語の雅楽「青海波」の装束に用いられたことでこの名がつき、江戸時代中期に広まりました。

Semicircles are repeated regularly in this auspicious pattern depicting rolling waves. It has been around since ancient times, but received its name (*seigaiha*, "blue ocean waves") from the attire worn during the imperial court music scene in the Tale of Genji. The pattern then spread during the middle of the Edo period.

23

はばたく鶴
Flapping Crane

胸部分を押さえながら尾を後ろに引くと、羽が上下にパタパタと動いてはばたきます。伝承折り紙のひとつで、動かして遊ぶ折り紙の代表例です。

If you hold onto the chest part and pull the tail backwards, the wings flutter up and down, as if to take flight. It is one of the traditional origami designs, and a typical example of origami that can be played with by producing movement.

p.75

鶴に遠波
Cranes Over Distant Waves

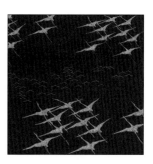

日本では7種類ほどの鶴が見られます。なかでも北海道に生息する丹頂鶴は神の使いとされ、信仰の対象となっていました。頭頂部が赤く美しい丹頂鶴の群れが、波を背景に飛ぶさまを描いています。

As many as seven different kinds of cranes can be seen in Japan. Among them, the red-crowned crane, which inhabits Hokkaido, came to be regarded as a messenger of gods and an object of faith. Here, a flock of beautiful red-crowned cranes are depicted soaring over a background of waves.

二重の鶴
Double-Layered Crane

基本の折り方を変えて作る、紙の裏面が見える鶴です。ツートンカラーになるため、表裏の色柄の違いが大きな紙で折ると、より華やかであざやかな鶴になります。

This crane, which shows the reverse side of the paper, is made by changing the basic folding instructions. Because the end result is two-toned, if the front and back patterns of the paper are very different, this crane becomes even more colorful and brilliant.

p.76

26

匠田小桜
<small>ひったこざくら</small>
Small *Hitta* Cherry Blossoms

「匹田」とは、絞り染めの匹田絞りからきた細かな紋様のこと。遠目には無地に見えて、実は細かな紋様があるという隠された贅沢が、江戸時代の着物柄として人気となっていました。

Hitta is a fine pattern that comes from a kind of tie-dying of the same name. The hidden luxury of its detailed design, which looks plain from afar, became popular as a pattern for kimono in the Edo period.

巣ごもり鶴
Nesting Crane

鶴は夫婦の絆が強く一生添いとげるといわれるため、円満な家庭の象徴ともされています。巣ごもり鶴は、卵をあたためる親鳥の姿を表わしています。

Cranes are also known to symbolize a happy home, as they are said to have strong bonds and mate for life. This nesting crane design shows a parent warming its eggs.

p.78

鮫小紋
Fine Sharkskin Pattern

一面に細かい紋様がつけられる小紋は、江戸時代には武士の正装である裃に用いられました。細かい点を同心円状に配した様子が鮫皮に見えることから、鮫小紋という呼び名がついています。

In the Edo period, fine patterns with detailed designs on one side were used in old ceremonial costumes worn by samurai as formal wear. This pattern gets its name from the similarity that the fine dots arranged in concentric circles have to sharkskin.

鶴の門松
かどまつ

Crane *Kadomatsu*

門松は、その年の福をもたらしてくれる歳神様を迎え入れるため門前に立てる、松や竹を用いた正月飾りです。折り紙の門松で、お正月らしさを演出しましょう。

A *kadomatsu* is a New Year's decoration made of pine or bamboo, placed in front of one's gate or door in order to welcome the deities who will bring good fortune in the year to come. Create an atmosphere fit for the New Year with this origami *kadomatsu*.

p.80

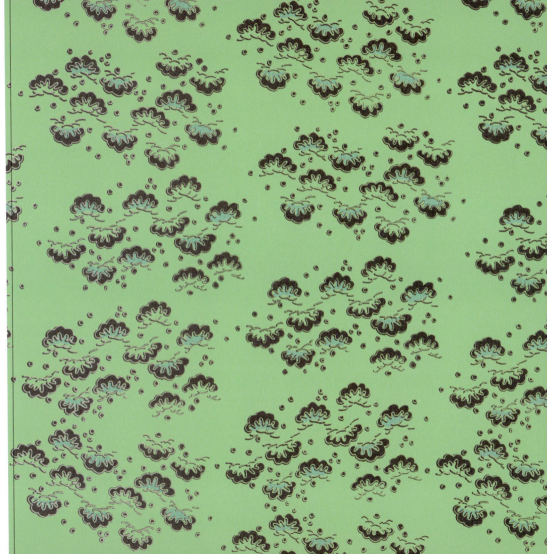

離れ三階松
Scattered Three-Tiered Pine

吉祥紋のひとつである松を用いた紋様です。松の枝が三層に重なったところを、横から見て図案化したもの。京都の北野天満宮では、梅鉢の紋様とともに神紋として使われています。

This pattern makes use of pine, another auspicious motif. It was designed to depict the view of pine branches overlapping in three layers as seen from the side. At Kitano Tenmangū in Kyoto, it is used as a shrine emblem, alongside the "plum bowl" motif.

31

<ruby>寿<rt>ことぶき</rt></ruby><ruby>鶴<rt>づる</rt></ruby> A
Congratulatory Crane A

新年や婚礼などのめでたいことを祝う「寿」の言葉を、縁起のいい鶴とかけた、おめでたい折り鶴です。お正月やお祝いの日に飾って楽しみましょう。

This special crane, in addition to being an omen of good luck itself, is filled with congratulations and best wishes for the New Year, for a wedding, or any happy celebration. Enjoy decorating with it for the New Year or other special occasions.

p.82

32

折り鶴
Paper Cranes

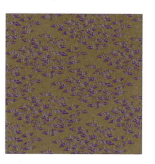

鶴だけでなく折り鶴も、着物や千代紙の柄に用いられるモチーフ。折り鶴をひし形に並べると、幾何学的なモダンな柄になります。鶴を折る女性が浮世絵などに登場する場合は、少女を表現しています。

In addition to actual cranes, paper cranes are also used as motifs for kimono and chiyogami patterns. Arranging these paper cranes into diamond shapes creates a modern geometric pattern. In *ukiyo-e* prints, if a young woman is seen folding a paper crane, it portrays her girlishness.

ことぶきづる
寿 鶴 B
Congratulatory Crane B

くじゃくのように羽を広げた形に折ることで、豪華な折り鶴になります。「寿鶴A」とは羽の折り方が異なり、また違った華やかさがあります。

Folding the feathers to spread out like a peacock's gives this paper crane its extravagance. Its wings are folded differently from Congratulatory Crane A, and it has a different kind of brilliance.

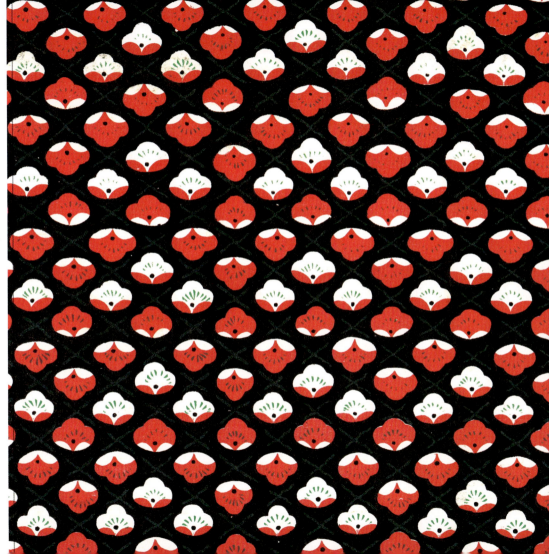

黒梅
Black Plum

梅の花はほかの花に先駆けて冬場に咲くことから、古くから愛され、多くの紋様に用いられています。黒地にひし形を配した図案に、白梅、紅梅が映える美しい紋様です。

Plum blossoms bloom in winter, ahead of other flowers, and so they have been loved since long ago, and used in many patterns. This is a beautiful pattern, with white and red plum blossoms set nicely against a design of diamonds over a black background.

35

鶴のめびな
Crane Empress Doll

3月3日の桃の節句は、女の子の成長を願うお祝いです。めびなとおびなのひな人形を鶴で折るのもよいでしょう。

Girls' Day on March 3rd is a celebration in hope for young girls' growth. Why not fold paper crane versions of the empress and emperor dolls?

p.88

宴姫
Princess's Banquet

十二単を身にまとった平安時代の姫たちが、満開の花をめでる宴を楽しんでいます。屏風から出てきたような美しい光景です。

These Heian princesses wearing 12-layered ceremonial kimono are enjoying a party while admiring the flowers in full bloom. It is a beautiful scene, as if having emerged from a folding screen.

37

鶴のおびな
Crane Emperor Doll

鶴のめびなとおびなを並べれば、長寿と幸福のイメージがふくらみます。一夫一妻の鶴にあやかり、結婚式の飾りにするのもおすすめです。

Set a crane empress doll next to a crane emperor doll, and the display will burst with an air of longevity and happiness. We also recommend them as wedding decorations, to share in the happy crane couple's good luck.

p.88

平安絵巻
Heian Picture Scroll

平安絵巻からの図柄です。全体にかかる雲の形は、画面に変化や遠近感を生むための「雲取り」といわれる紋様。現代も着物や帯によく見られます。

This design comes from a Heian period picture scroll. The pattern of cloud shapes covering the entire scene is called *kumodori*, a break in the clouds, used to create change or add the perception of depth to the scene. Even today, it can often be seen decorating kimono or obi.

端午の節句の鶴
Boys' Day Crane

5月5日の端午の節句では、男の子の健やかな成長を願って鎧兜や五月人形を飾る風習があります。はつらつと元気な折り鶴で祝いましょう。

For Boys' Day, there is a custom of decorating with armor or May dolls, while wishing for boys' health and growth. Celebrate the day with this lively and energetic paper crane.

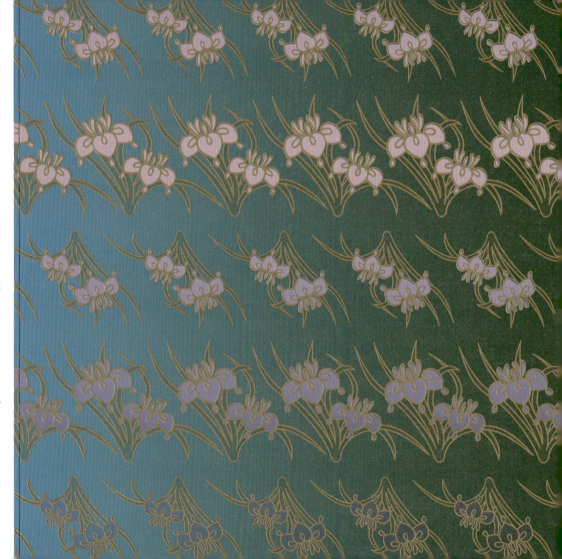

あやめ
Iris

端午の節句の時期に咲くあやめは、紫色の花びらの中心に網目模様が見られることから「あやめ」の名がついています。花菖蒲やかきつばたとよく似た花ですが、網目模様があることで区別することができます。

One species of Japanese iris, which blooms around Boys' Day, is called *ayame* in Japanese. The name comes from the word for mesh, *ayame*, since a mesh-like pattern can be seen in the center of the iris's purple petals. The flower is very similar to the Japanese water iris or rabbit-ear iris, but can be distinguished from the others by this mesh pattern.

鶴の器
Crane Bowl

安定感があるしっかりとした器になるので、ちょっとしたお菓子などを入れるのもよいでしょう。おもてなしのテーブルに、遊び心のある器として使えます。

This bowl is nice and stable, so it's perfect for placing small snacks inside. You can set this playful dish atop your table when entertaining guests.

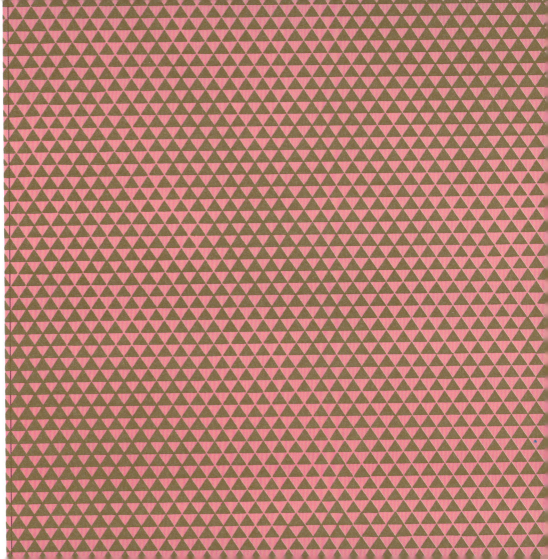

鱗
Scales

三角形が上下左右に連続した模様で、魚や蛇の鱗に見立てて名づけられています。江戸時代から歌舞伎の衣装にも見られ、能楽では蛇や鬼を表わす衣装によく使われます。

This pattern of repeating triangles in all directions is named for its similarity to the scales of fish and snakes. Since the Edo period, it has been seen in kabuki costumes, and has been often used for costumes representing snakes and demons in Noh theater.

小箱鶴
Small Box Crane

鶴のアレンジから、さまざまな器や入れ物も作ることができます。背中部分が箱になる小箱鶴は、小さなプレゼントを入れるのにもよいでしょう。

Various dishes and containers can be made from adapting the crane design. This crane, whose back opens up into a small box, is great for holding small gifts.

p.94

しだれ桜
Weeping Cherry

花びらを幾重にも重ねた八重のしだれ桜は、華やかさが魅力です。黒地に花が浮かび上がるデザインは、満開の夜桜を思わせます。

The double-flowered weeping cherry tree, whose petals overlap over and over again, charms the viewer with its gorgeousness. This design, in which flowers rise up out of the black background, evokes the sight of cherry blossoms at night in full bloom.

45

鶴の箸置き
Crane Chopstick Rest

本書の千代紙から4つの箸置きが作れます。いつもの食卓に添えるだけで、和を感じさせるおもてなしの演出ができます。

You can make four chopstick rests from chiyogami included in this book. Simply by arranging them on your dining table, you can create an air of hospitality that feels quite Japanese.

p.98

46

麻の葉
Hemp Leaves

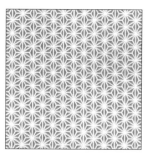

12個の三角形をぐるりと並べた正六角形の小紋柄。放射状に無限に連なる模様は光や仏の力を連想させて、平安・鎌倉時代の仏像の衣装などに使われ、江戸末期には一般にも広まりました。

This fine hexagonal pattern is created by arranging 12 triangles around a central point and repeating the motif. The never-ending radial pattern is associated with light and the power of Buddha, and was used for the clothing of Buddhist statues in the Heian and Kamakura periods. It was widespread in the late Edo period as well.

鶴の懐紙
Crane *Kaishi*

懐紙を鶴の形に作りました。お茶の席などで和菓子をのせるのはもちろん、クッキーやチョコレートをのせて洋風に使ってもよいでしょう。

This is a *kaishi*, a paper napkin used to serve sweets, folded in the shape of a crane. Of course, you can place Japanese sweets on it during a tea ceremony, but it may also be used to serve Western sweets like cookies or chocolate.

p.101

扇面流し
Floating Fans

扇は末広がりで縁起がよく、閉じたり開いたりと形の変化もあることから、よく使われるモチーフです。扇面流しは「川に落とした扇が流れる様子が美しかった」という故事に由来した紋様です。

Folding fans are often used as a motif, due to their versatility in depicting them open or closed, and as a sign of good luck (the phrase for "spreading out like an open fan" has a double meaning of "increasing prosperity"). The floating fan pattern comes from a story of someone who had dropped a fan into the river and noted how beautiful it looked floating downstream.

49

鶴のたとう
Crane *Tatō*

「たとう」とは畳み紙からきた言葉で、もともとは和紙を折りたたんで着物などをしまう包みのことをいいます。鶴のたとうは、お札や小さなメモなどを入れられます。

Tatō comes from the word for wrapping paper, and originally referred to a bundle or package made from washi paper to wrap and store kimono or other objects. This crane tatō can hold bills or small notes.

p.102

牡丹蝶
Butterflies & Peonies

蝶は、青虫から動かないさなぎになり蝶になる過程から、命がよみがえる吉祥の紋様とされています。不死不滅への願いから、武士が好んで使ったともいわれます。

The butterfly is an auspicious motif which represents the revival of life, as a caterpillar becomes an unmoving chrysalis, which then becomes a butterfly. It is said that samurai were fond of the motif and used it to symbolize their own desires for immortality and invincibility.

51

鶴のぽち袋 A
Crane *Pochi-bukuro* A

子どものお年玉など、少額のお金を入れて渡すための袋をぽち袋といいます。「これっぽっち」が語源という説があります。

The envelope used to gift small amounts of money to children, such as for New Year's, is called a *pochi-bukuro*. Some say the name comes from *koreppocchi*, meaning something small or paltry.

p.104

裾波に鶴
すそなみ
Crane Hemline Wave

飛び立つ鶴の群れと波をあしらった紋様。画面の下を中心に図柄を配置するのは、着物の柄と共通する描き方です。このように、波は鶴や千鳥などと組み合わせた紋様が多く見られます。

This pattern features a flock of cranes soaring over waves. Centering the design near the bottom is a style in common with kimono patterns. Many patterns like this can be seen, combining waves with cranes or other birds such as plovers.

鶴のぽち袋 B
Crane *Pochi-bukuro* B

鶴をあしらったかわいいぽち袋なら、ひと目でおめでたさが伝わります。ひと手間かけて、お祝いの気持ちを表現しましょう。

A cute *pochi-bukuro* featuring cranes will convey your congratulations at a single glance. Express your feelings of celebration with just a little time and effort.

p.107

亀甲花菱
Tortoise-shell Flower Crests

ひし形に描かれた花と亀甲模様を合わせた伝統的な紋様です。亀甲は正六角形をつなげた亀の甲羅のように見えるもので、亀にあやかる長寿の紋様といわれています。

This traditional design combines diamond-shaped flowers and a tortoise-shell pattern. The repeating hexagons look like the shells of tortoises strung together, creating an auspicious pattern said to represent the longevity associated with tortoises.

お祝い鶴
Celebratory Crane

祝儀袋の水引にも鶴の形があるように、鶴はお祝いごとに最適のモチーフです。厚みがない鶴なので、封筒などに貼って祝儀袋として使うこともできます。

The crane is the best motif for celebration, as can be seen by the crane-shaped *mizuhiki* decorations of congratulatory gift envelopes in Japan. Because this crane is not very thick, it can be attached to an envelope, to be used for presenting monetary gifts.

p.110

すそ鶴
Low-Flying Cranes

翼を広げて飛ぶ鶴の群れは、動きが大きい華やかな紋様となります。鶴は右側（上手）から左側（下手）に飛来する構図が一般的ですが、これは西方浄土を意味しているためです。

This flock of cranes spreading their wings to fly creates a gorgeous pattern with a great sense of movement. A common composition shows cranes flying from the upper right-hand side to the bottom left – this is in representation of the Western Pure Land of Buddhist mythology.

57

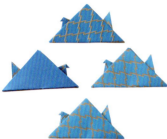

鶴のブックマーカー
Crane Corner Bookmarks

ページの隅にかぶせるタイプの個性的なブックマーカーです。さりげない鶴の形がかわいらしく、読書が楽しくなりそう。

These unique bookmarks cover the corner of the page. Their nonchalant crane shape is sweet, and sure to make reading even more enjoyable.

p.112

松の菱
Pine Diamonds

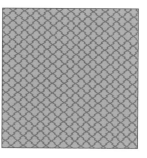

冬でも落葉せず風雪に耐えるため吉祥とされる松は、葉や枝振りなど多様な図案があります。この紋様は木の表面が割れる様子を模し、「松皮菱」とも呼ばれるもの。武士の羽織に用いられた紋様です。

There are a number of patterns featuring the leaves and branches of the pine tree, which is considered to be a lucky omen thanks to its ability to withstand wind and snow, and to never become bare, even in winter. This design imitates the cracking surface of the tree, and is also known as the pine bark pattern. It was used for samurai's formal coats (*haori*).

59

鶴のしおり
Crane Bookmark

基本の鶴を少しアレンジするだけで、しおりのできあがり。ページの上から、鶴が顔をのぞかせます。

By simply adapting the basic crane a little, this bookmark can be made. The crane's head is made to peek out from the top of the page.

p.113

しだれの桜
Weeping Cherry Blossoms

全面に咲くしだれ桜が小ぶりながらも美しい紋様です。平安時代にはすでに桜を鑑賞する風習があり、貴族が宴を催したといわれます。山桜から八重桜、しだれ桜と種類も増え、日本を代表する花となりました。

Weeping cherry blossoms bloom all over this design, creating a somewhat small, yet beautiful pattern. The custom of appreciating cherry blossoms had already been in place by the Heian period, and it is said that aristocrats would hold parties to do so. Varieties of cherry blossom trees increased, from mountain cherry to double-flowered and weeping cherry, and their flowers came to be representative of Japan itself.

61

鶴のメモスタンド
Crane Note Stand

長く伸びた羽部分にメモや写真などがはさめるスタンドです。メッセージを書いたカードを入れたりと、使い方はいろいろあります。

This stand can hold your notes or photos between its long, outstretched wings. Or place a handwritten card inside – there are lots of ways you can use it!

p.114

62

五崎し
Gokuzushi

そろばんよりも以前に計算に使われた算木を、5本ずつ市松模様に並べています。日常の道具で幾何学模様を作ったおもしろい紋様です。3本ずつは「三崎し」、4本ずつは「四崎し」と呼ばれます。

This design depicts counting rods, tools used for calculation even earlier than the abacus, arranged in a five-by-five checkered pattern. It is an interesting design, in which a geometric pattern has been created with everyday tools. The three-by-three version is called *sankuzushi*, and the four-by-four pattern, *yonkuzushi*.

63

鶴の花入れ
Crane Vase

鶴が前面についた三角の入れ物は、壁に貼るなどして使います。ドライフラワーを1枝入れたり、ヒモでいくつもつないで飾るのもおすすめです。

This triangular container with a crane on its front may be used by attaching it to a wall or other surface. We also recommend inserting a single dried flower, or stringing several together to decorate with.

p.116

64

枝梅
Plum Branches

中国から渡ってきた梅は『万葉集』にも多く詠まれ、平安時代以降、吉祥紋として親しまれてきました。花と小枝の明るい柄は、飾りものに最適です。

The plum, brought to Japan from China, was often written of in the Man'yōshū (the oldest existing collection of Japanese poetry), and since the Heian period, has become popular as an auspicious motif. This bright pattern of flowers and branches is perfect for decorations.

本書の作品の折り方

How to Fold Designs in This Book

Comment réaliser les différents origami de ce manuel :

本書中的作品摺法

基本の鶴
Basic Crane/Les bases du pliage de la Grue en origami/ 基本的紙鶴

難易度 /Difficulty/Difficulté/ 難度係數 ★☆☆

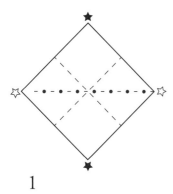

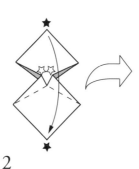

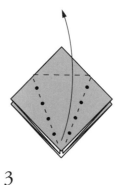

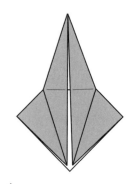

1

図のように折り筋をつける

Crease as shown in the diagram.

Marquez un pli comme sur le schéma.

如圖所示，摺出摺痕。

2

☆と☆、★と★がつくように、折り筋どおりにたたむ

Fold along the creases so that the points marked by star symbols (☆, ★) match up.

Pliez votre papier le long des lignes de façon à ce que les symboles ☆ et ★ se superposent.

☆和☆、★和★對齊，按照摺痕摺疊。

3

図のように折り筋をつけ、上の1枚を開いてたたむ

Crease as shown in the diagram, unfold the top layer and fold flat.

Marquez un pli comme sur le schéma, dépliez puis repliez la feuille supérieure.

如圖所示，摺出摺痕，攤開上方的1張摺疊。

4

たたんだところ。裏も同じに

It should look like this after folding. Repeat on the reverse side.

Une fois plié. Répétez la procédure pour la face inverse.

摺疊之後。背面也一樣。

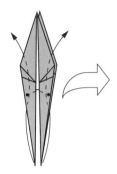

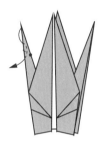

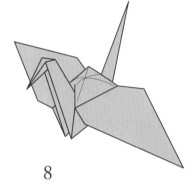

5

真ん中に合わせて折る。
裏も同じに

Fold to meet the center.
Repeat on the reverse side.

Pliez le papier en deux.
Répétez la procédure pour la face inverse.

對準正中央摺。背面也一樣。

6

左右を中割り折り(p.18)する

Inside reverse fold (p.18) on the left and right.

Faites un pli renversé intérieur de gauche à droite (p.18).

將左右往內翻摺(p.18)。

7

中割り折りして頭を作る

Inside reverse fold to make the head.

Faites un pli renversé intérieur pour réaliser la tête.

往內翻摺，製作鶴頭。

8

羽を広げて、できあがり

Spread out the wings, and it's finished!

Ouvrez les ailes... votre Grue est prête!

攤開翅膀，大工告成。

恋鶴
Love Cranes/Grue de l'amour/ 戀鶴
難易度 /Difficulty/Difficulté/ 難度係數 ★★☆

※縦：横が1：2の長方形の紙を用意する(本書では縦15cm×横30cmの和紙を使用)
Prepare a rectangular sheet of paper with a height: width ratio of 1:2 (this book uses 15x30 cm washi).
Préparez une feuille de papier rectangulaire (rapport longueur/largeur de 2:1).(Dans ce manuel nous utiliserons une feuille de papier japonais de 15 cm de largeur pour 30 cm de longueur.)
準備長：寬為1：2的長方形紙(本書中，使用長15cm×寬30cm 的和紙)。

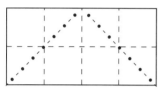

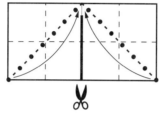

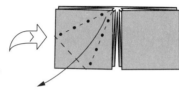

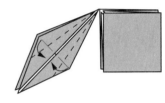

1
図のように折り筋をつける

Crease as shown in the diagram.

Marquez un pli comme sur le schéma.

如圖所示，摺出摺痕。

2
3〜5mm 残して中央に切りこみを入れ、折り筋どおりにたたむ

Cut in the center of the paper, leaving 3 – 5 mm of space. Fold along the creases.

Faites une incision au centre du rectangle en laissant une marge de 3 à 5 mm, puis pliez selon la ligne.

留下3〜5mm，往中央剪開，按照摺痕摺疊。

3
左側に図のように折り筋をつけ、上の1枚を開いてたたむ。裏も同じに

Crease as shown in the diagram to the left, unfold the top layer and fold flat. Repeat on the reverse side.

Marquez un pli sur le côté gauche comme sur le schéma, dépliez puis repliez la feuille supérieure. Répétez la procédure pour la face inverse.

如圖所示，在左側摺出摺痕，攤開上方的1張摺疊。背面也一樣。

4
「基本の鶴」(p.66) 5〜6と同様に折る

Fold in the same manner as in steps 5 & 6 of the Basic Crane (p.66).

Référez-vous aux points 5 à 6 de la section Les bases du pliage de la Grue (p.66).

和「基本的紙鶴」(p.66) 5〜6一樣摺。

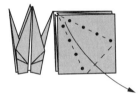

5

右側を3と同様に折る

Fold the right side in the same manner as in step 3.

Pliez le côté droit en vous référant au point 3.

將右側和3一樣摺。

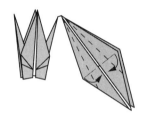

6

右側を「基本の鶴」5〜6と同様に折る

Fold the right side in the same manner as in steps 5 & 6 of the Basic Crane.

Pliez le côté droit en vous référant aux points 5 à 6 de la section Les bases du pliage de la Grue.

將右側和「基本的紙鶴」5〜6一樣摺。

7

くっついている側で、ともに中割り折り(p.18)して頭を作る

On the sides where the cranes are attached, fold both with an inside reverse fold (p.18) to make the heads.

Faites un pli renversé intérieur en joignant les côtés (p.18) pour réaliser la tête.

在連結側，左右都往內翻摺(p.18)，製成鶴頭。

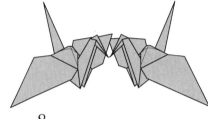

8

羽を広げて、できあがり

Spread out the wings, and it's finished!

Ouvrez les ailes... votre Grue est prête!

攤開翅膀，大工告成。

p.20

四連鶴
Quadruplet Cranes/Quatre Grues/ 四連鶴

難易度 /Difficulty/Difficulté/ 難度係數 ★★☆

※正方形の紙を用意する (本書では縦 30cm ×横 30cm の和紙を使用)
Prepare a square sheet of paper (this book uses 30x30 cm washi).
Préparez une feuille de format carré (Dans ce manuel nous utiliserons une feuille de papier japonais de 30 cm de largeur pour 30 cm de longueur).
準備正方形紙 (本書中，使用長 30cm× 寬 30cm 的和紙)。

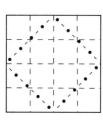

1

図のように折り筋をつける

Crease as shown in the diagram.

Marquez un pli comme sur le schéma.

如圖所示，摺出摺痕。

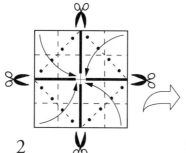

2

間を3〜5mm 残して、4か所に切りこみを入れる。折り筋どおりにたたむ。

Cut in four places, leaving 3 – 5 mm of space. Fold along the creases.

Coupez les quatre angles du carré en laissant une marge de 3 à 5 mm. Pliez selon les lignes.

將中間留下3〜5mm，在4處剪開。按照摺痕摺疊。

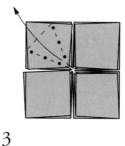

3

左上の四角に折り筋をつけ、開いてたたむ。裏も同じに

Crease the upper-left square as shown in the diagram. Unfold the top layer and fold flat.

Marquez les plis du carré supérieur gauche en vous référant au schéma, dépliez le papier du dessus puis repliez. Répétez la procédure pour la face inverse.

如圖所示，在左上方的角摺出摺痕，攤開上方的1張摺疊。背面也一樣。

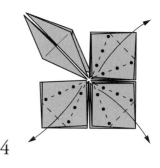

4

残りの3つも同様に折る

Fold the remaining three in the same manner.

Répétez la procédure pour les 3 autres carrés.

其餘3角也一樣摺。

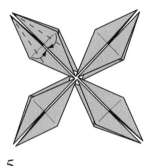

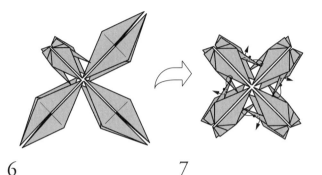

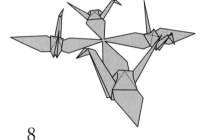

5

左上を図のように谷折りする。裏も同じに。両側を中割り折り(p.18)する

Valley fold the upper-left as shown in the diagram. Repeat on the reverse side, then inside reverse fold (p.18) both ends.

Faites un pli vallée pour la partie supérieure gauche en vous référant au tracé. Répétez la procédure pour la face inverse. Puis, faites un pli renversé intérieur sur les deux côtés (p.18).

如圖所示,將左上方谷摺。背面也一樣。然後,將兩側往內翻摺(p.18)。

6

残りの3つも同様に折る

Fold the remaining three in the same manner.

Répétez la procédure pour les 3 autres carrés.

其餘3角也一樣摺。

7

同じ向きに中割り折りして頭を作る

Make inside reverse folds to create the heads, all facing the same direction.

Faites un pli renversé intérieur dans la même direction pour réaliser la tête.

朝同方向往內翻摺,製作鶴頭。

8

羽を広げて、できあがり

Spread out the wings, and it's finished!

Ouvrez les ailes... votre Grue est prête!

攤開翅膀,大工告成。

青海波
Wave Pattern Cranes/Vagues bleues/青海波

難易度/Difficulty/Difficulté/難度係數 ★★★

※大きめの正方形の紙を用意する(本書では縦45cm×横45cmの和紙を使用)
Prepare a large square sheet of paper (this book uses 45x45 cm washi).
Préparez une large feuille de format carré (Dans ce manuel nous utiliserons une feuille de papier japonais de 45 cm de largeur pour 45 cm de longueur).
準備較大的正方形紙(本書中,使用長45cm×寬45cm的和紙)。

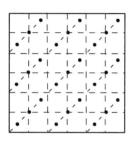

1

図のように折り筋をつける

Crease as shown in the diagram.

Marquez un pli comme sur le schéma.

如圖所示,摺出摺痕。

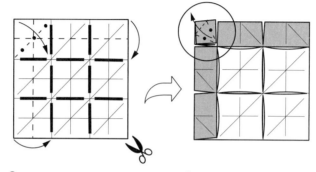

2

折り筋を利用し、それぞれ間を3〜5mm残して切りこみを入れる。左上の四角を折り筋どおりにたたむ

Make cuts along creases, leaving 3 – 5 mm of space. Fold the upper-left square flat along the creases.

Coupez selon les plis en laissant une marge de 3 à 5 mm. Pliez le carré supérieur gauche en suivant les lignes.

利用摺痕,將中間分別留下3〜5mm剪開。左上方的角按照摺痕摺疊。

3

左上の四角に図のように折り筋をつけ、上の1枚を開いてたたむ

Crease the upper-left square as shown in the diagram. Unfold the top layer and fold flat.

Marquez les plis du carré supérieur gauche en vous référant au schéma, dépliez le papier du dessus puis repliez.

如圖所示,在左上方的角摺出摺痕,攤開上方的1張摺疊。

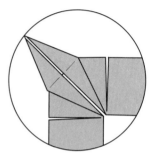

4

たたんだところ。裏も同じに

It should look like this after folding. Repeat on the reverse side.

Une fois plié. Répétez la procédure pour la face inverse.

摺疊之後。背面也一樣。

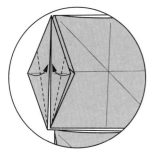
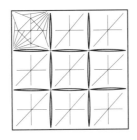
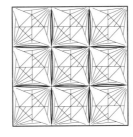
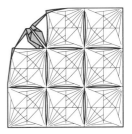

5

真ん中に合わせて谷折りする。裏も同様に折ってから、すべて開く

Meet edges in the middle and make a valley fold. After repeating on the reverse side, unfold everything.

Réalisez un pli vallée central. Pliez puis dépliez tout.

對準正中央谷摺。背面也一樣摺之後，全部攤開。

6

残り8つの四角も1つずつ、2〜5と同様に折って開くをくり返す

Repeat steps 2 – 5 for each of the remaining 8 squares.

Pliez et dépliez de façon répétée chacun des 8 carrés restants en vous référant aux points 2 à 5.

其餘8個角也一一和2〜5一樣反覆摺之後攤開。

7

9つすべて折り筋をつけたところ

It should look like this after creases have been made for all 9.

Une fois l'ensemble des neufs plis effectués.

9個角全部摺出摺痕之後。

8

左上の四角を折り筋どおりに折る

Fold the upper-left square along the creases.

Pliez le carré supérieur gauche selon les lignes.

左上方的角按照摺痕摺。

青海波 /Wave Pattern/Vagues bleues/ 青海波

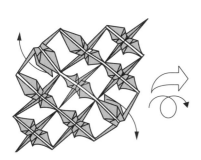
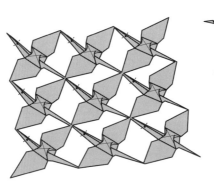

9

残り8つも折り筋どおりに折り、9羽折りあがったらすべて羽を広げる

Fold the remaining 8 along the creases. After all 9 have been folded, spread out all the wings.

Pliez également les 8 carrés restants selon les lignes, et ouvrez les ailes une fois le pliage aile 9 prêt.

其餘8個角也按照摺痕摺，9隻摺好之後，全部攤開翅膀。

10

すべて同じ向きに中割り折り(p.18)して頭を作る

Inside reverse fold (p.18) to make the heads, all facing the same direction.

Faites un pli renversé intérieur dans la même direction pour réaliser la tête (p.18).

全部朝同方向往內翻摺(p.18)，製作鶴頭。

11

できあがり

Finished!

C'est terminé.

大工告成。

はばたく鶴
Flapping Crane/Grue battant des ailes/ 振翅的鶴

難易度 /Difficulty/Difficulté/ 難度係數 ★ ☆ ☆

1

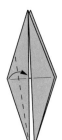

「基本の鶴」(p.66)の5から始める。片側のみ真ん中に合わせて谷折りする。裏も同じに

Start from step 5 of the Basic Crane (p.66). Fold only one side in to meet the center and valley fold. Repeat on the reverse side.

Commencez à partir de point 5 de la section Les bases du pliage de la Grue (p.66). Réalisez un pli vallée avec seulement un côté de la feuille. Répétez la procédure pour la face inverse.

從「基本的紙鶴」(p.66)的5開始。僅一側對準正中央谷摺。背面也一樣。

2

中割り折り(p.18)する

Inside reverse fold (p.18).

Faites un pli renversé intérieur (p.18).

往內翻摺(p.18)。

3

中割り折りして頭を作る

Inside reverse fold to make the head.

Faites un pli renversé intérieur pour réaliser la tête.

往內翻摺・製作鶴頭。

4

中割り折りで尾を水平に折る

Fold the tail horizontally using an inside reverse fold.

Pliez la queue à l'horizontal via un pli renversé intérieur.

往內翻摺・將尾巴水平摺。

5

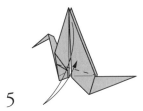

羽の根元で折り筋をつける。裏も同じに

Crease at the base of the wings.

Marquez un pli à la base des ailes (répétez la procédure pour la face inverse).

在翅膀的根部摺出摺痕。背面也一樣。

6

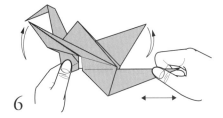

できあがり。図のように持って尾を引くと、羽がパタパタと動く

Finishet! Hold as shown in the diagram, and pull on the tail to make the wings flap.

C'est terminé. En tirant la queue comme sur le schéma, les ailes se mettent à battre !

大工告成。如圖所示,拿在手中,拉扯尾巴,就會鼓動翅膀。

p.23

二重の鶴
Double-Layered Crane/Deux Grues/ 雙層鶴

難易度 /Difficulty/Difficulté/ 難度係數 ★☆☆

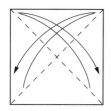

1

図のように折り筋をつける

Crease as shown in the diagram.

Marquez un pli comme sur le schéma.

如圖所示，摺出摺痕。

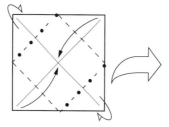

2

中心に向かって、それぞれ谷折り、山折りする

Make valley and mountain folds toward the center.

Réalisez un pli montagne puis un pli vallée.

朝中心點分別谷摺、山摺。

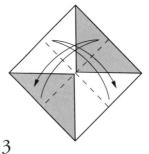

3

谷折りの折り筋をつける

Crease with the valley fold.

Marquez le pli vallée.

摺出谷摺的摺痕。

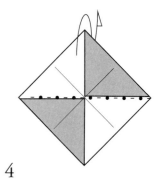

4

山折りの折り筋をつける

Crease with the mountain fold.

Marquez le pli montagne.

摺出山摺的摺痕。

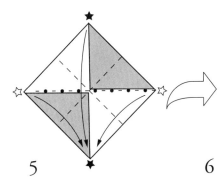

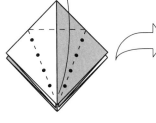

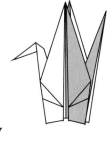

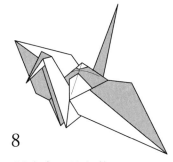

5

☆と☆、★と★がつくように、折り筋どおりにたたむ

Fold flat along the creases, making sure the points marked by star symbols (☆, ★) meet.

Pliez votre papier le long des lignes de façon à ce que les symboles ☆ et ★ se superposent.

☆和☆、★和★對齊，按照摺痕摺疊。

6

「基本の鶴」(p.66)3〜7と同様に折る

Fold in the same manner as in steps 3 – 7 of the Basic Crane (p.66).

Réalisez ce modèle en vous référant aux points 3 à 7 de la section Les bases du pliage de la Grue (p.66).

和「基本的紙鶴」(p.66)3〜7一樣摺。

7

折り終わったところ

It should look like this when finished.

Une fois le pliage terminé.

摺完之後。

8

羽を広げて、できあがり

Spread out the wings, and it's finished!

Ouvrez les ailes... votre Grue est prête!

攤開翅膀，大工告成。

巣ごもり鶴
Nesting Crane / Nid de la Grue / 抱窩的鶴

難易度 /Difficulty/Difficulté/ 難度係數 ★☆☆

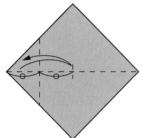

1

図のように折り筋をつける

Crease as shown in the diagram.

Marquez un pli comme sur le schéma.

如圖所示，摺出摺痕。

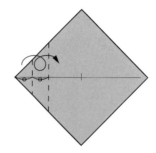

2

左側を巻き折り(p.18)する

Roll fold (p.18) the left side.

Pliez en enroulant la partie gauche de votre feuille (p.18).

將左側卷摺(p.18)。

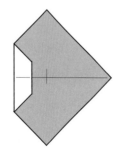

3

折ったところ。裏返して向きを変える

It should look like this after folding. Turn over and rotate.

Une fois plié. Retournez la feuille et changez de direction.

摺好之後。翻面，改變方向。

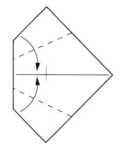

4

真ん中に合わせて谷折りする

Meet edges in the middle and valley fold.

Réalisez un pli vallée au center.

對準正中央谷摺。

5

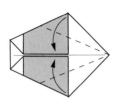

もう一度、真ん中に合わせて谷折りする

Once more, meet edges in the middle and valley fold.

Réalisez à nouveau un pli vallée au center.

再次對準正中央谷摺。

6

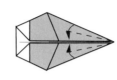

真ん中に合わせて、途中まで谷折りする

Meet edges in the middle and valley fold up to the halfway point.

Réalisez un pli vallée central partiel.

對準正中央,對半谷摺。

7

図の位置で山折りし、裏返す

Mountain fold at the point shown in the diagram, and turn over.

Réalisez un pli montagne selon la position indiquée par le tracé puis retournez la feuille.

在圖中的位置山摺,翻面。

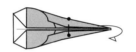

8

谷折りして頭を作る

Make the head with a valley fold.

Réalisez un pli vallée pour faire la tête.

谷摺,製作鶴頭。

9

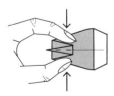

頭をおさえて、体を丸く整える

Push down the head, and adjust the body to make it round.

Ajustez le corps de la grue tout en la tenant par la tête.

按住鶴頭,將身體弄圓。

10

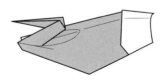

できあがり

Finished!

C'est terminé.

大工告成。

p.27

鶴の門松

Crane *Kadomatsu*/Grue Kadomatsu/ 鶴的門松

難易度 /Difficulty/Difficulté/ 難度係數 ★☆☆

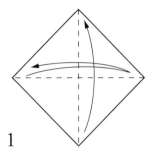

1

図のように折り筋をつけ、半分に谷折りする

Crease as shown in the diagram, then valley fold in half.

Marquez un pli comme sur le schéma, et faites un pli vallée avec la moitié de la feuille.

如圖所示，摺出摺痕，對半谷摺。

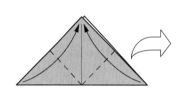

2

両側の角を折り上げる

Fold the corners up on both sides.

Pliez tous les coins de chaque côté de la feuille.

將兩側的角往上摺。

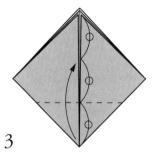

3

3分の1の位置で谷折りする

Valley fold one-third of the paper.

Réalisez un pli vallée jusqu'au tiers.

在3分之1的位置谷摺。

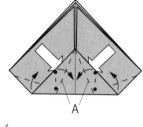

4

Aの折り筋をつけ、Aを谷折りしながら開いてつぶす

Make creases for A. While valley folding A, unfold and squash flat.

Marquez le pli A, puis tout en réalisant un pli vallée dépliez et pressez.

摺出 A 的摺痕，一面將 A 谷摺，一面攤開壓平。

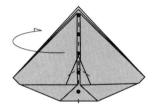

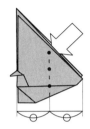

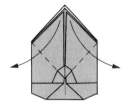

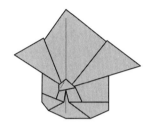

5

全体を半分に山折りしながら、かぶせ折り(p.18)で頭を作る

While mountain folding everything in half, make the head with an outside reverse fold (p.18).

Tout en réalisant un pli montagne avec la moitié de la feuille, faites un pli renversé extérieur (p.18) pour réaliser la tête.

一面將整體對半山摺，一面向外翻摺(p.18)，製作鶴頭。

6

半分の位置で山折りする。裏も同じに

Mountain fold at the halfway point. Repeat on the reverse side.

Réalisez un pli montagne à partir de la moitié. Répétez la procédure pour la face inverse.

在一半的位置山摺。背面也一樣。

7

上から1枚を谷折りする

Valley fold the top layer.

Réalisez un pli vallée depuis le haut d'une feuille.

從上方將1張谷摺。

8

できあがり

Finished!

C'est terminé.

大工告成。

p.29

寿鶴 A
Congratulatory Crane A/Grue Célébration A/ 壽鶴 A

難易度 /Difficulty/Difficulté/ 難度係數 ★★☆

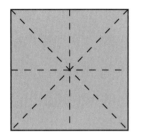

1

図のように折り筋をつける

Crease as shown in the diagram.

Marquez un pli comme sur le schéma.

如圖所示，摺出摺痕。

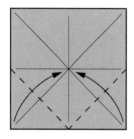

2

両側を三角に谷折りする

Valley fold both sides into a triangle.

Faites un pli vallée en triangle avec les deux côtés de la feuille.

將兩側谷摺成三角形。

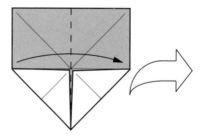

3

半分に折る

Fold in half.

Pliez en deux.

對摺。

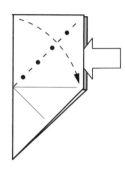

4

間を開いて中割り折り(p.18)する

Unfold the space and make an inside reverse fold (p.18).

Dépliez l'intervalle et faites pli renversé intérieur (p.18).

攤開中間，往內翻摺(p.18)。

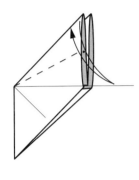

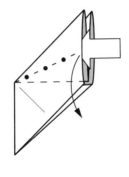

5

上の1組に折り筋をつける。
裏も同じに

Crease the top set of layers.
Repeat on the reverse side.

Marquez les plis pour l'ensemble supérieur. Répétez la procédure pour la face inverse.

在上方的1組摺出摺痕。背面也一樣。

6

間を開いてつぶす。裏も同じに

Unfold the space and squash flat. Repeat on the reverse side.

Dépliez l'intervalle puis presses. Répétez la procédure pour la face inverse.

攤開中間壓平。背面也一樣。

7

図の位置で谷折りする。
裏も同じに

Valley fold at the point shown in the diagram. Repeat on the reverse side.

Réalisez un pli vallée selon la position indiquée par les traces. Répétez la procédure pour la face inverse.

在圖中的位置谷摺。背面也一樣。

8

半分に折る。裏も同じに

Fold in half. Repeat on the reverse side.

Pliez en deux. Répétez la procédure pour la face inverse.

對摺。背面也一樣。

寿鶴 A/Congratulatory Crane A/Grue Célébration A/ 壽鶴 A

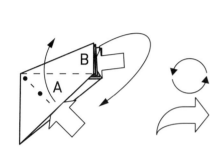
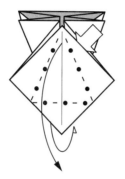
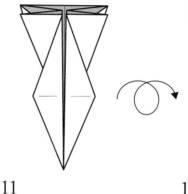

9

Aは間を開いてつぶす。Bは下の2組を折り下げる

For A, unfold the space and squash flat. For B, fold down the bottom two sets of layers.

Pour A, dépliez l'intervalle puis pressez. Pour B, pliez les deux ensembles inférieurs vers le bas.

A 攤開中間壓平。B 將下方的2組往下摺。

10

図のように折り筋をつけ、開いて折りたたむ

Crease as shown in the diagram, unfold and fold flat.

Marquez les plis selon le tracé et dépliez et repliez.

如圖所示，摺出摺痕，攤開摺疊。

11

たたんだところ。裏返す

It should look like this after folding. Turn over.

Une fois plié. Retournez.

摺疊之後。翻面。

12

半分に折る

Fold in half.

Pliez en deux.

對摺。

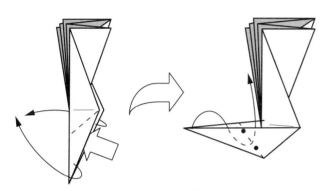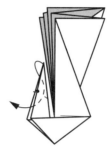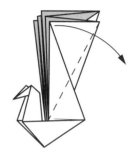

13

折り筋をつけて、かぶせ折り (p.18)する

Crease and outside reverse fold (p.18).

Marquez un pli puis faites un pli renversé extérieur (p.18).

摺出摺痕,往外翻摺(p.18)。

14

中割り折り(p.18)する

Make an inside reverse fold (p.18).

Faites un pli renversé intérieur (p.18).

往內翻摺(p.18)。

15

中割り折りして頭を作る

Inside reverse fold to make the head.

Faites un pli renversé intérieur pour réaliser la tête.

往內翻摺,製作鶴頭。

16

羽の、上の1枚を谷折りして開く。裏も同じに

Valley fold the top layer of the wings and unfold them.

Réalisez un pli vallée pour la feuille supérieure des ailes puis dépliez. Répétez la procédure pour la face inverse.

將翅膀上方的1張谷摺攤開。背面也一樣。

寿鶴 A/Congratulatory Crane A/Grue Célébration A/ 壽鶴 A

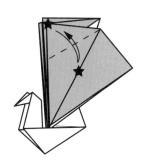 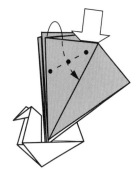 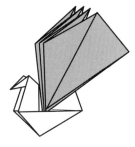 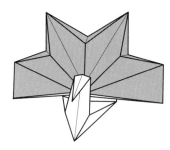

17

上の1組を、★と★がつくように折り筋をつける

Crease the top set of layers so that the ★ marks align.

Marquez les plis de l'ensemble supérieur afin que les symboles ★ se superposent.

★和★對齊，將上方的1組摺出摺痕。

18

間を開いて中割り折りする。
ほかの2組も同じに

Unfold the space and inside reverse fold. Fold the other two sets of layers in the same manner.

Dépliez l'intervalle puis faites un pli renversé intérieur. Répétez la procédure pour les deux autres ensembles.

攤開中間，往內翻摺。其他2組也一樣。

19

折ったところ

It should look like this when folded.

Une fois plié.

摺好之後。

20

羽を広げて、できあがり

Spread out the wings, and it's finished!

Ouvrez les ailes... votre Grue est prête!

攤開翅膀，大工告成。

寿鶴 B
Congratulatory Crane B/Grue Célébration B/ 壽鶴 B

難易度 /Difficulty/Difficulté/ 難度係數 ★★☆

1
「寿鶴 A」(p.82)の16から始める。上の1組を、★と★がつくように折り筋をつける

Start from step 16 of Congratulatory Crane A (p. 82). Crease the top set of layers so that the ★ marks align.

Commencez par le point 16 de la partie Grue Célébration A (p.82). Marquez les plis de l'ensemble supérieur afin que les symboles ★ se superposent.

從「壽鶴 A」(p.82)的16開始。★和★對齊,將上方的1組摺出摺痕。

2
間を開いて中割り折り(p.18)する

Unfold the space and inside reverse fold (p.18).

Dépliez l'intervalle et faites pli renversé intérieur (p.18).

攤開中間,往內翻摺(p.18)。

3
他の3組も同様に折る

Fold the other three sets of layers in the same manner.

Répétez la même procédure pour les 3 autres ensembles.

其他3組也一樣摺。

4
折ったところ

It should look like this after folding.

Une fois plié.

摺好之後。

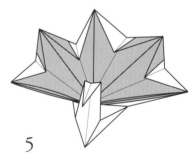

5
羽を広げて、できあがり

Spread out the wings, and it's finished!

Ouvrez les ailes... votre Grue est prête!

攤開翅膀,大工告成。

p.33

鶴のめびな・おびな
Crane Empress Doll and Emperor Doll / Les poupées Mebina et Obina de la Grue / 皇后鶴、天皇鶴

難易度 /Difficulty/Difficulté/ 難度係數 ★☆☆

1

「端午の節句の鶴」(p.90)の3から始める。上の1枚を折り下げる

Start from step 3 of the Boys' Day Crane (p.90). Fold down the top layer.

Commencez par le point 3 de la partie Festival Tango Grue (p.90). Pliez la feuille supérieure vers le bas.

從「端午節的鶴」(p.90)的3開始。將上方的1張往下摺。

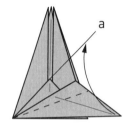

2

補助線 a に合わせて折り上げる

Match with guide line 'a' and fold up.

Pliez selon la ligne auxiliaire a.

對準輔助線 a 往上摺。

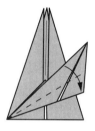

3

半分に谷折りする

Valley fold in half.

Réalisez un pli vallée jusqu'à la moitié.

對半谷摺。

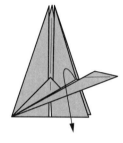

4

まとめて折り下げる

Fold down all at once.

Assemblez et pliez.

整個往下摺。

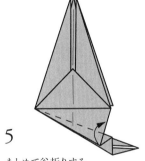

5

まとめて谷折りする

Valley fold all at once.

Assemblez et réalisez un pli vallée.

整個谷摺。

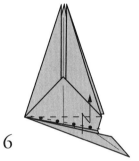

6

まとめて段折り(p.18)する。
裏も1〜6と同様に折る

Pleat fold (p.18) all at once. Fold the reverse side in the same manner, following steps 1 – 6.

Réalisez un pliage général en accordéon (p.18). Pour la partie opposée, pliez en vous référant aux points 1 à 6.

整個段摺(p.18)。背面也和1〜6一樣摺。

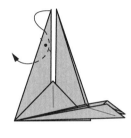

7

中割り折り(p.18)して頭を作る

Inside reverse fold (p.18) to make the head.

Faites un pli renversé intérieur pour réaliser la tête (p.18).

往內翻摺(p.18),製作鶴頭。

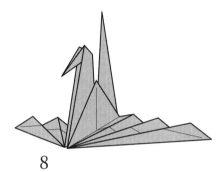

8

羽を広げて、できあがり

Spread out the wings, and it's finished!

Ouvrez les ailes... votre Grue est prête!

攤開翅膀,大工告成。

p.35,37

端午の節句の鶴
Boys' Day Crane/Festival Tango Grue/ 端午節的鶴

難易度 /Difficulty/Difficulté/ 難度係數 ★☆☆

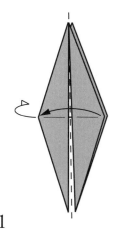

1

「基本の鶴」(p.66)の5から始める。
上の1枚を左へ折る。裏も同じに

Start from step 5 of the Basic Crane (p.66). Fold the top layer to the left. Repeat on the reverse side.

Commencez à partir du point 5 de la partie Les bases du pliage de la Grue (p.66). Répétez la procédure pour la face inverse.

從「基本的紙鶴」(p.66)的5開始。將上方的1張往左摺。背面也一樣。

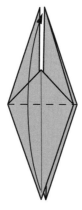

2

上の1枚を折り上げる。裏も同じに

Fold the top layer up at the point shown in the diagram. Repeat on the reverse side.

Pliez la feuille supérieure selon la position indiquée par le tracé. Répétez la procédure pour la face inverse.

將上方的1張在圖中的位置往上摺。背面也一樣。

3

図の位置で開きながら、折り筋どおりにたたむ。裏も同じに

While unfolding at the point shown in the diagram, fold flat along the creases. Repeat on the reverse side.

Pliez selon les lignes tout en dépliant comme indiqué par les positions des tracés. Répétez la procédure pour la face inverse.

一面在圖中的位置攤開,一面按照摺痕摺疊。背面也一樣。

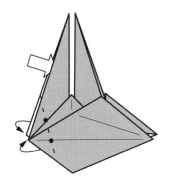
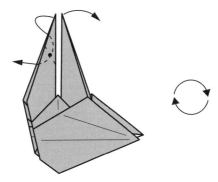
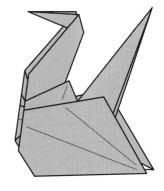

4

図の位置で内側に山折りする。
裏も同じに

Mountain fold inside at the point shown in the diagram. Repeat on the reverse side.

Réalisez un pli montagne interne selon la position indiquée par les tracés. Répétez la procédure pour la face inverse.

在圖中的位置往內側山摺。背面也一樣。

5

中割り折り(p.18)して頭を作る。
尾を後ろに引く

Inside reverse fold (p.18) to make the head. Pull tail backwards.

Faites un pli renversé intérieur (p.18) pour réaliser la tête. Tirez la queue vers l'arrière.

往內翻摺(p.18),製作鶴頭。將尾巴往後拉。

6

できあがり

Finished!

C' est terminé.

大工告成。

p.39

鶴の器
Crane Bowl/Boîte Grue/ 鶴的容器

難易度 /Difficulty/Difficulté/ 難度係數 ★★☆

1

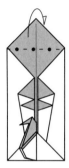

「鶴のぽち袋 B」(p.107)の17から始める(器の中面に模様がくるように、紙の表と裏を折り図と逆にして折る)。図の位置で山折りする

Start from step 17 of Crane *Pochi-bukuro* B (p.107). (For the inside of the bowl to show the patterned side of the paper, reverse the front and back sides as seen in the diagrams.) Mountain fold at the point shown in the diagram.

Commencez par le point 17 de la partie Enveloppe Grue B(p.107). (Pliez les deux faces de la feuille, puis une nouvelle fois de manière inverse au tracé, afin que le motif s'ajuste sur la surface centrale de la partie récipient). Faites un pli montagne en vous référant au tracé.

從「鶴的小袋子 B」(p.107)的17開始(為了讓圖案出現在容器的內側，將紙的正面和背面跟摺紙圖相反摺)。在圖中的位置山摺。

2

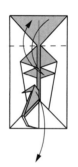

谷折りして折り筋をつける。鶴部分をまとめて折り下げる

Valley fold to crease. Fold the crane part down all at once.

Réalisez un pli vallée et marquez un pli. Pliez vers le bas toutes les parties de la grue.

谷摺摺出摺痕。將鶴的部分整個往下摺。

3

開きながら箱型を作る

Make a box shop while unfolding.

Formez la boite en dépliant.

一面攤開，一面製作盒子的形狀。

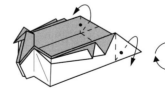

4

後ろを図のように折る

Fold the back as shown in the diagram.

Pliez l' arrière comme sur le schema.

將後方如圖所示摺。

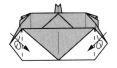

5

後ろの三角部分を巻き折り(p.18)してまとめる

Roll fold (p.18) the triangular part of the back and bring everything together.

Pliez en enroulant pour joindre les parties triangulaires arrières (p.18).

將後方的三角部分卷摺(p.18)。

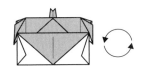

6

折ったところ

It should look like this after folding.

Une fois plié.

摺好之後。

7

羽を広げ、後ろの三角の尾を水平にする

Spread out the wings and make the triangular tail at the back horizontal.

Déployez les ailes, puis ajustez la queue triangulaire arrière à l'horizontal.

攤開翅膀，將後方的三角形尾巴弄成水平。

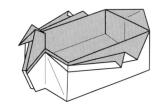

8

できあがり

Finished!

C' est terminé.

大工告成。

小箱鶴
Small Box Crane/Petite boîte Grue/ 小盒子鶴

難易度 /Difficulty/Difficulté/ 難度係數 ★★☆

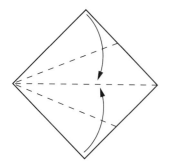

1

三角に折り筋をつけ、
折り筋に合わせて谷折りする

Crease in a triangular shape, then align the creases and valley fold.

Marquez les plis du triangle puis réalisez un pli vallée selon ces plis.

摺出三角形的摺痕‧對準摺痕谷摺。

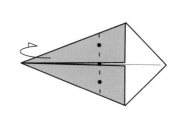

2

半分に山折りする

Mountain fold in half.

Réalisez un pli montagne jusqu'à la moitié.

對半山摺。

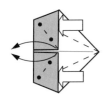

3

間を開いてたたむ

Unfold the space and fold flat.

Dépliez l'intervalle puis repliez.

攤開中間摺疊。

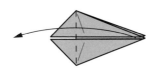

4

上の1組を左へ開く

Unfold the top set of layers to the left.

Dépliez l'ensemble supérieur vers la gauche.

將上方的1組往左攤開。

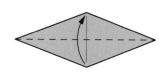

5

半分に谷折りする

Valley fold in half.

Réalisez un pli vallée jusqu'à la moitié.

對半谷摺。

6

図のように折り筋をつけ、間を開いてつぶす

Crease as shown in the diagram, unfold the space and squash flat.

Marquez les plis selon le tracé, dépliez l'intervalle puis presses.

如圖所示，摺出摺痕，攤開中間壓平。

7

図のように折り筋をつける

Crease as shown in the diagram.

Marquez un pli comme sur le schéma.

如圖所示，摺出摺痕。

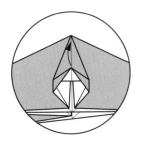

8

7でつけた折り筋で山折りにし、上に開いて折りたたむ。裏も6〜8と同様に折る

Mountain fold along the creases made in step 7, unfold towards the top and fold flat. Fold the reverse side in the same manner, following steps 6 – 8.

Faites un pli montagne sur la ligne réalisée au point 7, puis dépliez vers le haut avant de replier. Pour la face inverse, pliez de la même façon en vous référant aux points 6 à 8.

以在7摺出的摺痕山摺，往上攤開摺疊。背面也和6〜8一樣摺。

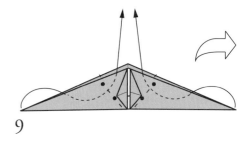

9

左右を大きく中割り折り(p.18)する

Make large inside reverse folds (p.18) on the left and right.

Faites un large pli renversé intérieur de gauche à droite (p.18).

將左右大大地往內翻摺(p.18)。

小箱鶴 /Small Box Crane/Petite boîte Grue/ 小盒子鶴

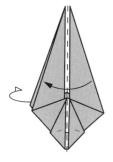

10

右上の1組を左に折る。
裏も同じに

Fold the top-right set of layers to the left. Repeat on the reverse side.

Pliez le côté supérieur droit de l'ensemble vers la gauche. Répétez la procédure pour la face inverse.

將右上方的1組往左摺。背面也一樣。

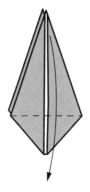

11

谷折りして折り下げる。
裏も同じに

Valley fold and fold down. Repeat on the reverse side.

Réalisez un pli vallée et pliez vers le bas. Répétez la procédure pour la face inverse.

谷摺往下摺。背面也一樣。

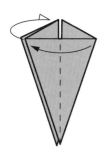

12

右上の1組を左に折る。
裏も同じに

Fold the top right set of layers to the left. Repeat on the reverse side.

Pliez le côté supérieur droit de l'ensemble vers la gauche. Répétez la procédure pour la face inverse

谷摺往下摺。背面也一樣。

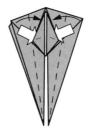

13

両側を半分に折って差し入れる。
裏も同じに

Fold both sides in half, and insert at the point shown in the diagram. Repeat on the reverse side.

Pliez chaque côté jusqu'à la moitié, avant d'insérer selon le tracé. Répétez la procédure pour la face inverse.

將兩側對摺，插入圖中的位置。背面也一樣。

14

左右を中割り折りする

Make inside reverse folds on the left and right.

Faites un pli renversé intérieur vers la gauche et la droite.

將左右往內翻摺。

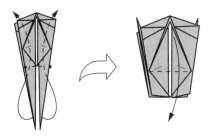

15

羽根を折り下げる。
裏も同じに

Fold down the base of the wing. Repeat on the reverse side.

Pliez les ailes vers le bas. Répétez la procédure pour la face inverse.

將翅膀往下摺。背面也一樣。

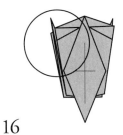

16

中割り折りして頭を作る

Inside reverse fold to make the head.

Faites un pli renversé intérieur pour réaliser la tête.

往內翻摺，製作鶴頭。

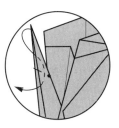

17

折っているところ

It should look like this when folded.

Une fois plié.

摺的時候。

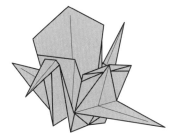

18

箱を広げ、形を整えてできあがり

Open up the box and adjust the shape. Finished!

Arrangez la forme de la boîte. C'est terminé!

攤開盒子，調整形狀，大工告成。

p.43

鶴の箸置き
Crane Chopstick Rest/Porte-baguettes Grue/ 鶴的筷架

難易度 /Difficulty/Difficulté/ 難度係數 ★★☆

※紙をキリトリ線で4つに切って作る
Cut into four pieces along the dotted lines to make.
Découpez la feuille en 4 parties le long des pointillés.
以虛線將紙剪成4張製作。

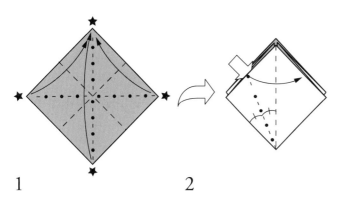
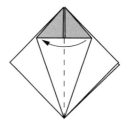
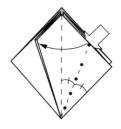

1
図のように折り筋をつけ、★を合わせるように折りたたむ

Crease as shown in the diagram and fold flat, making sure that the ★ marks align.

Marquez les plis selon le tracé, puis pliez de façon à ce que les symboles ★ se superposent.

如圖所示，摺出摺痕，對齊★摺疊。

2
上の1組の間を開いてつぶす

Unfold the space between the top set of layers and squash flat.

Dépliez puis froissez les intervalles de l'ensemble supérieur.

攤開上方的1組中間壓平。

3
上の1枚を左へ折る

Fold the top layer to the left.

Pliez la feuille supérieure vers la gauche.

將上方的1張往左摺。

4
右側の1組も同様に開いてつぶし、上の1枚を右に折る

Unfold and squash flat the set of layers on the right side in the same manner, and fold the top layer to the right.

Faites de même pour l'ensemble du côté droit, avant de plier la feuille supérieure vers la droite.

右側的1組也一樣攤開壓平，將上方的1張往右摺。

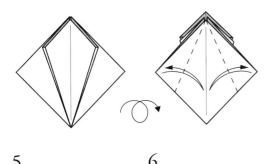

5

折ったところ。裏返す

It should look like this when folded. Turn over.

Une fois plié. Retournez.

摺好之後。翻面。

6

図のように折り筋をつける

Crease as shown in the diagram.

Marquez un pli comme sur le schéma.

如圖所示，摺出摺痕。

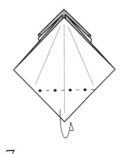

7

下を山折りする

Mountain fold the bottom.

Réalisez un pli montagne avec la partie inférieure.

將下方山摺。

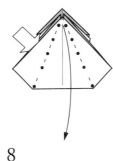

8

折り筋どおりに開いてたたむ

Crease, then unfold and fold flat along the creases.

Marquez les plis, puis dépliez et repliez selon les lignes.

摺出摺痕，按照摺痕攤開折疊。

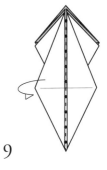

9

全体を半分に山折りする

Mountain fold everything in half.

Réalisez un pli montagne jusqu'à la moitié.

將整體對半山摺。

鶴の箸置き/Crane Chopstick Rest/Porte-baguettes Grue/ 鶴的筷架

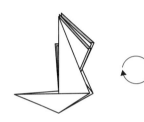

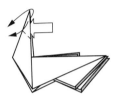

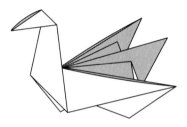

10

折り筋をつけてかぶせ折り(p.18)する

Crease and make outside reverse fold (p.18).

Marquez les plis puis faites un pli renversé extérieur (p.18).

摺出摺痕，往外翻摺(p.18)。

11

折ったところ。向きを変える

It should look like this when folded. Rotate.

Une fois plié. Changez le sens.

摺好之後。改變方向。

12

かぶせ折りして頭を作る

Outside reverse fold to make the head.

Faites un pli renversé extérieur pour réaliser la tête.

往外翻摺，製作鶴頭。

13

羽を広げて、できあがり

Spread out the wings, and it's finished!

Ouvrez les ailes... votre Grue est prête!

攤開翅膀，大工告成。

p.45

鶴の懐紙
Crane *Kaishi* /Feuille de papier Grue/ 鶴的懷紙

難易度/Difficulty ★★★

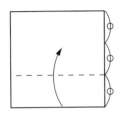

1

3分の1の位置で谷折りする

Valley fold one-third of the paper.

Réalisez un pli vallée jusqu'au tiers.

在3分之1的位置谷摺。

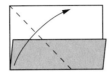

2

三角に谷折りする

Valley fold into a triangle.

Faites un pli vallée en triangle.

谷摺成三角形。

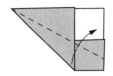

3

図の位置で谷折りする

Valley fold at the point shown in the diagram.

Réalisez un pli montagne selon le trace.

在圖中的位置谷摺。

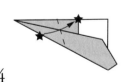

4

★と★がつくように谷折りする

Valley fold so that the ★ marks align.

Réalisez un pli vallée de façon à ce que les symboles ★ se superposent.

★和★對齊谷摺。

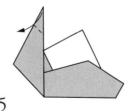

5

谷折りして頭を作る

Make the head with a valley fold.

Réalisez un pli vallée pour faire la tête.

谷摺・製作鶴頭。

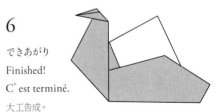

6

できあがり

Finished!

C'est terminé.

大工告成。

p.47

鶴のたとう
Crane Tatō /Carte Grue/ 鶴的疊紙

難易度 /Difficulty/Difficulté/ 難度係數 ★☆☆

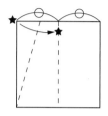

1

半分に折って中心線を作り、
★と★がつくように谷折りする

Fold in half to make a center line, then valley fold so that the ★ marks align.

Pliez jusqu'à la moitié afin de former la ligne centrale, puis réalisez un pli vallée afin que les symboles ★ se superposent.

對摺，製作中心線，★和★對齊谷摺。

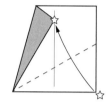

2

☆と☆がつくように谷折りする

Valley fold so that the ☆ marks align.

Réalisez un pli vallée de façon à ce que les symboles ☆ se superposent.

☆和☆對齊谷摺。

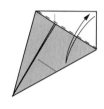

3

図のように折り筋をつける

Crease as shown in the diagram.

Marquez un pli comme sur le schéma.

如圖所示，摺出摺痕。

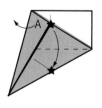

4

★と★がつくように谷折りする。Aを開く

Valley fold so that the ★ marks align. Unfold A.

Réalisez un pli vallée de façon à ce que les symboles ★ se superposent. Dépliez A.

★和★對齊谷摺。攤開 A。

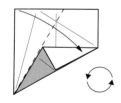

5

図のように谷折りする

Valley fold as shown in the diagram.

Réalisez un pli vallée comme sur le schema.

如圖所示，谷摺。

6

上の1枚を谷折り

Valley fold the top layer.

Faites un pli vallée pour la feuille supérieure.

將上方的1張谷摺。

7

図のように谷折りする

Valley fold as shown in the diagram.

Réalisez un pli vallée comme sur le schema.

如圖所示，谷摺。

8

図の位置で谷折りし、間を開いて差し入れる

Valley fold at the point shown in the diagram, unfold the space and insert.

Réalisez un pli vallée selon le tracé, dépliez l'intervalle puis insérez.

在圖中的位置谷摺，攤開中間插入。

9

半分に折り上げる

Fold up in half.

Pliez jusqu'à la moitié.

往上對摺。

10

谷折りして頭を作る

Make the head with a valley fold.

Réalisez un pli vallée pour faire la tête.

谷摺，製作鶴頭。

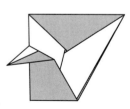

11

できあがり

Finished!

C' est terminé.

大工告成。

p.49

鶴のぽち袋 A
Crane *Pochi-bukuro* A/Enveloppe Grue A/ 鶴的小袋子 A

難易度 /Difficulty/Difficulté/ 難度係數 ★★☆

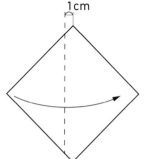

1
真ん中から1cm 左の位置で谷折りする

Valley fold on the left, 1 cm from the center.

Faites un pli vallée, 1 cm sur la gauche à partir du centre.

在正中央往左1cm 的位置谷摺。

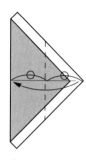

2
半分に谷折りする

Valley fold in half.

Réalisez un pli vallée jusqu'à la moitié.

對半谷摺。

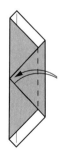

3
上の1枚のみ折り筋をつけ、すべて開く

Crease only the top layer, then unfold everything.

Marquez les plis de feuille supérieure uniquement, puis dépliez le tout.

僅上方的1張摺出摺痕,全部攤開。

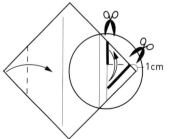

4
左側は折り筋に合わせて谷折りする。
右側は図のように切りこみを入れる

On the left side, valley fold along the crease. On the right side, cut as shown in the diagram.

Réalisez un pli vallée pour le côté gauche selon les lignes de pli. Coupez et insérez la partie droite comme indiqué sur le schema.

左側對準摺痕谷摺。右側如圖所示,剪開。

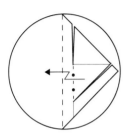

5

図のように段折り(p.18)する

Pleat fold (p.18) as shown in the diagram.

Faites un pli en accordéon selon le tracé (p.18).

如圖所示・段摺(p.18)。

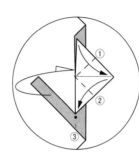

6

①②の順で谷折りする。
③は山折りして中に入れる

Valley fold ①, then ②. Mountain fold ③ and tuck inside.

Faites un pli vallée dans l'ordre 1 et 2. Faites un pli montagne pour la partie 3 puis insérez au milieu.

按照①②的順序谷摺。③山摺・放進裡面。

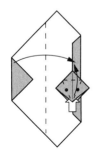

7

折り筋に合わせて谷折りし、右側の下に入れこむ。
右側の四角部分は折り筋をつけて開いてたたむ

Valley fold along the crease, and insert the right side into the bottom. Crease the square on the right side, unfold and fold flat.

Faites un pli vallée selon les lignes, puis insérez dans la partie inférieure du côté droit. Dépliez puis repliez les parties carrées du côté droit après avoir marqué les plis.

對準摺痕谷摺・放進右側的下方。右側的四角部分摺出摺痕・攤開摺疊。

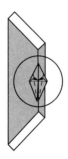

8

真ん中に合わせて谷折り

Align with the center and valley fold.

Réalisez un pli vallée central.

對準正中央谷摺。

鶴のぽち袋 A/Crane *Pochi-bukuro* A/Enveloppe Grue A/ 鶴的小袋子 A

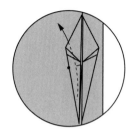

9

首部分を山折りする

Mountain fold the neck.

Faites un pli montagne pour la partie cou.

將脖子部分山摺。

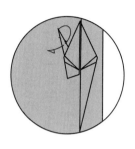

10

山折りして頭を作る

Mountain fold to make the head.

Faites un pli montagne pour réaliser la tête.

山摺‧製作鶴頭。

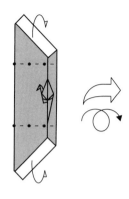

11

上下を山折りし、後ろで差しこむ

Mountain fold the top and bottom, and tuck in at the back.

Faites un pli montagne de haut en bas, puis insérez à l'arrière.

將上下山摺‧在後方插入。

12

差しこんだところ

It should look like this after tucking in.

Une fois inséré.

插入之後。

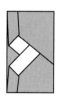

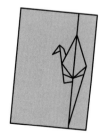

13

できあがり

Finished!

C' est terminé.

大工告成。

p.51

鶴のぽち袋 B

Crane *Pochi-bukuro* B/ Enveloppe Grue B/ 鶴的小袋子 B

難易度 /Difficulty/Difficulté/ 難度係數 ★★☆

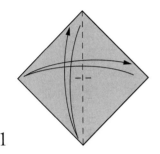

1

図のように折り筋をつけ、紙の中心の印をつける

Crease as shown in the diagram, and mark the center of the paper.

Marquez les plis selon le tracé, puis faites une marque au centre de la feuille.

如圖所示，摺出摺痕，在紙的中心點做記號。

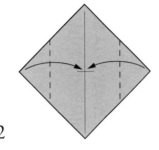

2

真ん中に合わせて両側を谷折りし、裏返す

Meet edges in the middle and valley fold both sides. Turn over.

Réalisez un pli vallée central avec les deux côtés de la feuille. Retournez.

將兩側對準正中央谷摺，翻面。

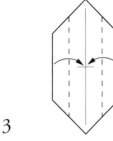

3

上の1枚のみ谷折りする

Valley fold only the top layer.

Réalisez un pli vallée avec la feuille supérieure uniquement.

僅上方的1張谷摺。

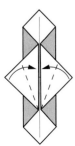

4

図のように谷折りする

Valley fold as shown in the diagram.

Réalisez un pli vallée comme sur le schema.

如圖所示，谷摺。

5

さらに谷折りする

Valley fold again.

Réalisez à nouveau un pli vallée.

再次谷摺。

6

4〜5で折ったところを開く

Unfold the folds made in steps 4 and 5.

Dépliez ce que vous avez plié lors des points 4 et 5.

將在4〜5摺好部分攤開。

鶴のぽち袋 B/Crane *Pochi-bukuro* B/Enveloppe Grue B/ 鶴的小袋子 B

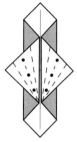

7
折り筋を折り直しながらたたむ

Readjust the creases as you fold flat.

Pliez selon les lignes tout en ajustant.

一面重新摺出摺痕，一面摺疊。

8
折りたたんだところ

It should look like this after folding.

Une fois plié.

摺疊之後。

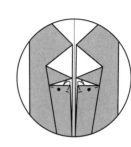

9
端を少し山折りして折りこむ

Mountain fold the edge slightly and fold inside.

Réalisez un léger pli montagne sur le bord.

將邊緣稍微山摺，摺進去。

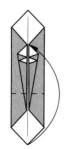

10
まとめて折り上げる

Fold up all at once.

Pliez vers le haut.

整個往上摺。

11
上の1組のみ折り筋をつける

Crease only the top set of layers.

Marquez un pli pour l'ensemble supérieur seulement.

僅上方的1組摺出摺痕。

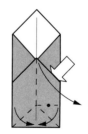

12
折り筋どおりにたたむ

Fold flat along the creases.

Pliez selon la ligne.

按照摺痕摺疊。

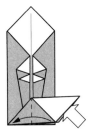

13

間を開いてたたむ

Unfold the space and fold flat.

Dépliez l'intervalle puis repliez.

攤開中間摺疊。

14

折り筋をつけて鶴を折る

Crease and fold the crane.

Marquez les plis puis pliez la grue.

摺出摺痕，摺紙鶴。

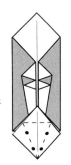

15

鶴部分を左に折る

Fold the crane part to the left.

Pliez les parties de la grue vers la gauche.

將鶴的部分往左摺。

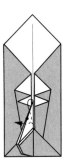

16

中割り折り(p.18)して頭を作る

Inside reverse fold (p.18) to make the head.

Faites un pli renversé intérieur pour réaliser la tête (p.18).

往內翻摺(p.18)，製作鶴頭。

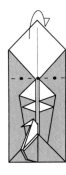

17

図の位置で山折りする

Mountain fold at the point shown in the diagram.

Réalisez un pli montagne comme indiqué sur le schema.

在圖中的位置山摺。

18

できあがり

Finished!

C'est terminé.

大工告成。

お祝い鶴
Celebratory Crane/Célébration Grue/ 喜慶的鶴

難易度 /Difficulty/Difficulté/ 難度係數 ★☆☆

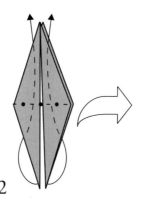

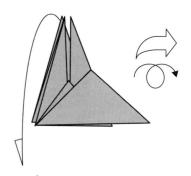

1

「基本の鶴」(p.66)の5から始める

Start from step 5 of the Basic Crane (p.66).

Commencez à partir de point 5 de la section Les bases du pliage de la Grue (p.66).

從「基本的紙鶴」(p.66)的5開始。

2

両側を中割り折り(p.18)する

Inside reverse fold (p.18) on both sides.

Faites un pli renversé intérieur avec les deux côtés (p.18).

將兩側往內翻摺(p.18)。

3

図のように谷折りする

Valley fold as shown in the diagram.

Réalisez un pli vallée comme sur le schema.

如圖所示，谷摺。

4

裏は下に折り下げる。裏返す

Fold down the reverse side toward the bottom. Turn over.

Pliez l'autre côté de la feuille vers le bas. Retournez.

背面往下摺。翻面。

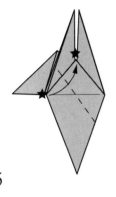
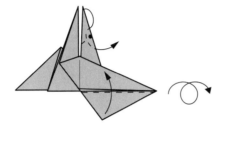
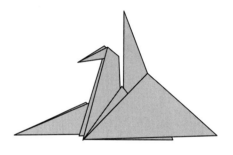

5

★と★がつくように谷折りする

Valley fold so that the ★ marks align.

Réalisez un pli vallée de façon à ce que les symboles ★ se superposent.

★和★對齊谷摺。

6

中割り折りして頭を作る。羽を折り上げる

Inside reverse fold to make the head. Fold the wings up.

Faites un pli renversé pour réaliser la tête. Pliez les ailes.

往內翻摺，製作鶴頭。將翅膀往上摺。

7

できあがり

Finished!

C'est terminé.

大工告成。

p.55

鶴のブックマーカー
Crane Corner Bookmarks/Bookmark Grue/ 鶴的書籤套夾

難易度 /Difficulty/Difficulté/ 難度係數 ★☆☆

※紙をキリトリ線で4つに切って作る
Cut into four pieces along the dotted lines to make.
Découpez la feuille en 4 parties le long des pointillés.
以虛線將紙剪成4張製作。

1

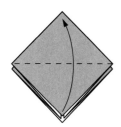

「基本の鶴」(p.66)の2から始める。
上の1枚のみ折り上げる

Start from step 2 of the Basic Crane (p.66). Fold only the top layer up.

Commencez à partir de point 2 de la section Les bases du pliage de la Grue (p.66). Pliez uniquement la feuille du haut vers le haut.

從「基本的紙鶴」(p.66)的2開始。僅上方的1張往上摺。

2

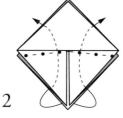

左右を中割り折り(p.18)する

Inside reverse fold (p.18) the left and right.

Faites un pli renversé intérieur de gauche à droite (p.18).

將左右往內翻摺(p.18)。

3

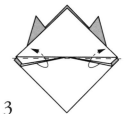

2組まとめて谷折りし、中に折りこむ

Valley fold two sets of layers all at once, then fold inside.

Assemblez les deux ensembles par un pli vallée, puis pliez/insérez au center.

2組一起谷摺,摺進裡面。

4

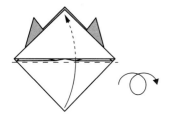

後ろの1枚も谷折りし、中に折りこむ。裏返す

Valley fold the back layer and fold inside as well. Turn over.

Pliez également l'arrière de la feuille puis pliez/insérez au centre. Retournez.

後方的1張也谷摺,摺進裡面。翻面。

5

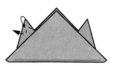

中割り折りして頭を作る

Inside reverse fold to make the head.

Faites un pli renversé intérieur pour réaliser la tête.

往內翻摺,製作鶴頭。

6

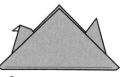

できあがり

Finished!

C'est terminé.

大工告成。

 p.57

鶴のしおり
Crane Bookmark/Marque-page Grue/ 鶴的書籤

難易度 /Difficulty/Difficulté/ 難度係數 ★☆☆

1

「基本の鶴」(p.66)の6から始める。
片側のみ中割り折り(p.18)する

Start from step 6 of the Basic Crane (p.66). Inside reverse fold (p.18) only one side.

Commencez à partir de point 6 de la section Les bases du pliage de la Grue (p.66). Faites un pli renversé intérieur avec un seul des côtés (p.18).

從「基本的紙鶴」(p.66)的6開始。左側谷摺，右側山摺，然後攤開。背面也一樣。

2

上の羽のみ谷折りする

Valley fold the top wing only.

Faites un pli vallée avec le haut des ailes seulement.

僅上方的翅膀谷摺。

3

中割り折りして頭を作る

Inside reverse fold to make the head.

Faites un pli renversé intérieur pour réaliser la tête.

往內翻摺，製作鶴頭。

4

できあがり

Finished!

C'est terminé.

大工告成。

p.59

鶴のメモスタンド

Crane Note Stand/Porte memo Grue/ 鶴的便條紙立架

難易度 /Difficulty ★☆☆

1

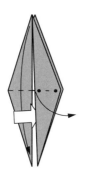

「基本の鶴」(p.66)の5から始める。
左側は谷折り、右側は山折りしながら開く。裏も同じに

Start from step 5 of the Basic Crane (p.66). Valley fold the left side. While mountain folding the right side, unfold. Repeat on the reverse side.

Commencez à partir de point 5 de la section Les bases du pliage de la Grue (p.66). Faites un pli vallée pour le côté gauche, puis dépliez en réalisant un pli montagne du côté droit. Répétez la procédure pour la face inverse.

從「基本的紙鶴」(p.66)的5開始。左側谷摺，右側山摺，然後攤開。背面也一樣。

2

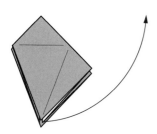

上から2枚目の角を引き出す

Pull out the corner of the second layer from the top.

Tirez les coins de la seconde feuille en partant du haut.

從上方拉出第2張的角。

3

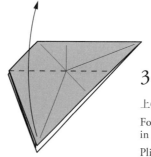

上の1枚のみ図の位置で折り上げる。裏も同じに

Fold only the top layer up, at the point shown in the diagram. Repeat on the reverse side.

Pliez vers le haut la feuille supérieure uniquement, comme sur le trace. Répétez la procédure pour la face inverse.

僅上方的1張在圖中的位置往上摺。背面也一樣。

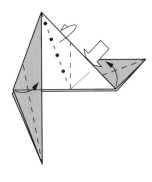

4

左側は半分に谷折りする。右側は間を開いて図のように谷折りと山折りをし、中へ折りこむ。裏も同じに

Valley fold the left side in half. On the right side, unfold the space and valley fold and mountain fold as shown in the diagram. Fold inside. Repeat on the reverse side.

Réalisez un pli vallée du côté gauche jusqu'à sa moitié. Pour le côté droit, dépliez l'intervalle puis faites des plis vallée et montagne selon le tracé avant de replier/insérer vers le centre. Répétez la procédure pour la face inverse.

左側對半谷摺。右側攤開中間，如圖所示，谷摺和山摺，摺進裡面。背面也一樣。

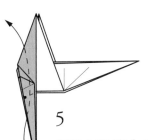

5

左側を中割り折り(p.18)する

Inside reverse fold (p.18) the left side.

Réalisez un pli renversé intérieur avec le côté gauche (p.18).

將左側往內翻摺(p.18)。

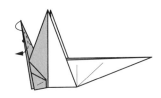

6

中割り折りして頭を作る

Inside reverse fold to make the head.

Faites un pli renversé intérieur pour réaliser la tête.

往內翻摺，製作鶴頭。

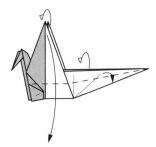

7

羽を折り下げ、続けて尾も半分に折る。裏も同じに

Fold down the wings and fold the tail in half. Repeat on the reverse side.

Pliez les ailes vers le bas, puis pliez également la queue jusqu'à la moitié. Répétez la procédure pour la face inverse.

將翅膀往下摺，接著尾巴也對摺。背面也一樣。

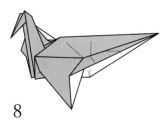

8

羽を水平にして、できあがり

Make the wings horizontal, and it's finished!

Pliez les ailes à l'horizontal. C'est terminé!

將翅膀弄成水平，大工告成。

p.61

鶴の花入れ
Crane Vase/Vase Grue/ 鶴的花瓶
難易度 /Difficulty/Difficulté/ 難度係數 ★★☆

1

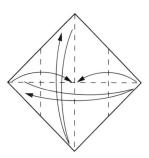

図のように折り筋をつけ、両側を三角に折る

Crease as shown in the diagram, then fold both sides into a triangle.

Marquez les plis selon le tracé, puis pliez en triangle de chaque côté.

如圖所示，摺出摺痕，將兩側摺成三角形。

2

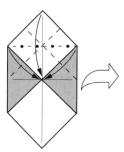

図のように折り筋をつけ、折り筋どおりにたたむ

Crease as shown in the diagram, then fold flat along the creases.

Marquez un pli comme sur le schéma puis pliez en suivant les lignes.

如圖所示，摺出摺痕，按照摺痕摺疊。

3

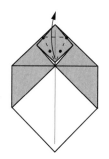

折り筋をつけ、開いてたたむ

Crease, unfold and fold flat.

Marquez un pli et dépliez avant de replier.

摺出摺痕，攤開摺疊。

4

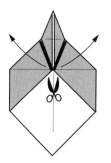

図の位置で上の1枚にのみ切りこみを入れて開く

Cut only the top layer at the point shown in the diagram and unfold.

Coupez uniquement la feuille supérieure selon le tracé, puis dépliez.

在圖中的位置，僅上方的1張剪開，攤開。

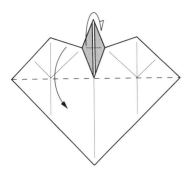

5

真ん中で谷折りし、
鶴部分は後ろに倒す

Valley fold at the middle and move the crane part down towards the back.

Faites un pli vallée central, puis rabattez les parties de la grue à l'arrière.

在正中央谷摺，鶴的部分往後弄倒。

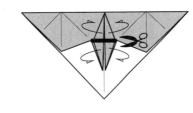

6

鶴部分の上の1枚に切りこみを入れ、裏に折り返す

Cut the top layer of the crane and fold back.

Coupez la feuille supérieure des parties de la grue, puis repliez vers la face opposée.

鶴的部分上方的1張剪開，往後翻摺。

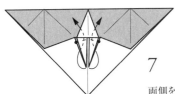

7

両側を中割り折り(p.18)する

Inside reverse fold (p.18) on both sides.

Faites un pli renversé intérieur avec les deux côtés (p.18).

將兩側往內翻摺(p.18)。

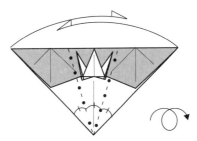

8

角度を3等分して山折りし、裏返す

Divide into three equal parts and mountain fold. Turn over.

Faites un pli montagne après avoir diviser les angles en trois parties. Retournez.

將角度分成3等分山摺，翻面。

鶴の花入れ /Crane Vase/Vase Grue/ 鶴的花瓶

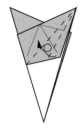

9

上の1枚を巻き折り(p.18)する

Roll fold (p.18) the top layer.

Pliez la feuille supérieure en enroulant (p.18).

將上方的1張卷摺(p.18)。

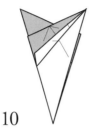

10

折ったところ。裏返す

It should look like this when folded. Turn over.

Une fois plié. Retournez.

摺好之後。翻面。

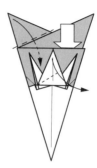

11

図の位置で谷折りして中に入れる。
鶴の羽を斜めに折り下げる

Valley fold at the point shown in the diagram and tuck inside. Fold down the crane's wing at a slant.

Réalisez un pli vallée selon le tracé puis insérez au centre. Pliez les ailes de la Grue en diagonale vers le bas.

在圖中的位置谷摺，放進裡面。將鶴的翅膀往斜下方摺。

12

中割り折りして頭を作る

Inside reverse fold to make the head.

Faites un pli renversé intérieur pour réaliser la tête.

往內翻摺，製作鶴頭。

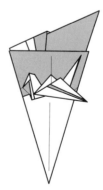

13

できあがり

Finished!

C'est terminé.

大工告成。

小林一夫

1941年、東京・湯島に生まれる。東京にある「お茶の水 おりがみ会館」館長。安政5年(1858年)創業の和紙の老舗「ゆしまの小林」4代目、会長。
NPO法人国際おりがみ協会理事長。折り紙の展示や、教室の開催、講演などを通じ、和紙文化の普及と継承に力を注いでいる。折り紙を本格的に折り始めたのは30代から。特に先人の知恵や技を感じることのできる伝承の折り紙を愛し、古くから日本人の心に根ざし、生活の中にある折り紙のあり方を伝播させている。
その活動場所は日本のみならず世界各国に及び、日本文化の紹介、国際交流にもつとめている。
著書に『英訳付き おりがみBOOK』(二見書房)、『折り紙は泣いている』(愛育社)、『折り、願い、遊ぶ―折紙の文化史』(里文出版)など多数。

Kazuo Kobayashi

Born in Yushima, Tokyo, in 1941, Kazuo Kobayashi is director of Ochanomizu Origami Kaikan, located in Ochanomizu, Tokyo. He is the fourth and chairman of the long-standing washi shop, Yushima no Kobayashi (est. 1858). Kobayashi also works to popularize and pass on washi culture and traditions by holding exhibitions, seminars and lectures in his role as Director of the International Origami Society, an NPO corporation. He began creating his own origami works in earnest while in his thirties. Kobayashi's deepest passion is passing on origami traditions that feature the wisdom and unique skill of the ancients, and propagate the role of origami in everyday life rooted in the hearts and minds of the Japanese people for centuries. Active not only in Japan, Kobayashi travels worldwide to showcase Japanese culture and promote international exchange. He has published many books, Including Origami Handbook with English translation(published by Futami shobo),Origami wa Naiteiru (Origami is Crying) (published by Aiikusya), and Cultural History of ORIGAMI(Ribun Publications).Kobayashi has also acted as a supervising editor for many publications about Origami.

作品制作	渡部浩美
折り図作成	岩田ワレス奈穂子
デザイン	ヤマシタツトム
撮影	寺岡みゆき
スタイリング・執筆協力	宮野明子
翻訳	トライベクトル株式会社
編集協力	河英実（おりがみ会館）
千代紙協力	寿工藝(p.37)、お茶の水 おりがみ会館（ゆしまの小林）

鶴のおりがみBOOK

著者　小林一夫（こばやしかずお）

発行　株式会社 二見書房
　　　東京都千代田区神田三崎町2-18-11
　　　電話 03(3515)2311[営業]
　　　　　 03(3515)2313[編集]
　　　振替 00170-4-2639

印刷・製本　TOPPANクロレ株式会社

落丁・乱丁がありました場合は、おとりかえします。
定価はカバーに表示してあります。
©Kazuo Kobayashi, 2018. Printed in Japan
ISBN978-4-576-18120-2
http://www.futami.co.jp